Contemporary Swedish Poetry

Contemporary Swedish Poetry

Translated by John Matthias
and Göran Printz-Påhlson

THE SWALLOW PRESS INC.
CHICAGO

Copyright © 1980 by John Matthias & Göran Printz-Påhlson
All Rights Reserved
Printed in England

Published by
The Swallow Press Incorporated
811 W. Junior Terrace
Chicago, Illinois 60613

First Printing 1980

Library of Congress Catalog Card Number: 79-9655
ISBN 0-8040-0811-6 cloth
ISBN 0-8040-0812-4 paper

Contents

Introduction by Göran Printz-Påhlson   9

Note by John Matthias   17

   I *Do you know the country?*

       LARS FORSSELL
          Sweden in the Summer   21

       LASSE SÖDERBERG
          The Capital of Fear   23

       GÖRAN PALM
          On This Earth   25

       SONJA ÅKESSON
          A Letter   29

       TOMAS TRANSTRÖMER
          Baltic Seas III   33

   II *Anthology*

       INGEMAR LECKIUS
          On Another Planet   39
          Family Life   39
          Magister Caput   40
          Paul Klee   41
          Mirobolus Makadam & Co.   43
          Speakers in Tongues   43
          Metaphysics   44
          To a Zen Monk   44
          The Voyeurs of Suffering   45
          In the Desert the Wild Sheep Roam   45
          Scintilla Animae   46

       MAJKEN JOHANSSON
          Little Dialectic for Poets   47
          A House of Gertrude Stein   47
          Gertrude Stein Again   48
          René Descartes   48
          Excursion   49
          A Meditation   50
          To the Forbears   50

Contents

    The Demons 51
    Elegy at a Grave 52
    Staircase 54
    Nostalgic Letter to G. P.-P. 54

GÖRAN PRINTZ-PÅHLSON
    Broendal 57
    Two Prose Poems 57
    Three Baroque Arias *from* Gradiva 58
    Sir Charles Babbage Returns . . . 61
    Man-Made Monster . . . 61
    Turing Machine 62
    Joe Hill in Prison 63

GÖRAN SONNEVI
    Abstract World 65
    Unfinished 65
    Lake and Silence 65
    Landscape 66
    February: Abstract Awakening 66
    'Void which falls out of void . . .' 67
    Hölderlin I 67
    Hölderlin II 68
    Will You Please Come In and Put on a Hat! 70
    'Bloody cunt! . . .' 71
    After Seven Lean Years 72
    It Has to Work 73
    'A mother stands in front . . .' 74
    Mozart Variations 75

GÖSTA FRIBERG
    Nobody 81
    The House of the Deaf and Dumb 81
    The Road 82
    The Growing 84

TOBIAS BERGGREN
    Poem from Gotland, 1 Sept. '73 89
    In the Mountain: Part II 90
    Poem about Time, by the Sea 94

LARS NORÉN
    Solitary Poem 99
    Syringe 100

Contents

    31 Words about Flanders   100
    From Dresden   101
    I Burn My Lamp in the Meadow   101
    Today, the Rage for Harmony   101
    Evening   102
    The Sphere of the Roads   102
    Allusions   102
    Endpoem   103
    Conclusion   103
    August   104
    from Wednesday October 17th   105

JAN ÖSTERGREN
    Words   109
    Love   111
    Death   114

PETER ORTMAN
    Naughtnaught   117
    Certain Days   117
    Prose Poem   118
    Prose Poem   119
    Realism   119
    Nothing Particular   120

JACQUES WERUP
    Poet Tranströmer and the Rest of Us   123
    'I could just as well go somewhere else'   124
    from Spots, Life   125

Notes on the Poets   131

Acknowledgements   134

Introduction / The Tradition of Contemporary Swedish Poetry

'. . . and what are poets for in a destitute time?' was a question asked by Hölderlin in a famous elegy, a question which prompted one of Heidegger's most penetrating late essays. *Wozu Dichter* is a question of perennial importance. 'What are poets for in an affluent land?' might be suggested as a possible emendation, perhaps more pertinent to our times and our culture, and in particular to a country like Sweden which has for many years suffered from a reputation (albeit largely unearned) for almost inhuman levels of social efficiency. It is somehow easier to accept that good poetry should arise from political upheaval and turbulence or from material privation than from the secure contentment of superb social engineering.

It is nevertheless a commonplace of much longer standing that the most durable tradition of Swedish literature has been a predominantly lyrical one, and that consequently the subtleties of rhythm and imagery inherent in the genius of poetry have fared less well in translation than, let us say, the subtleties of thought and observation illuminating the high points of the literatures of the other Scandinavian countries—in Kierkegaard or Ibsen, for instance. This may come as a surprise to the casual observer who has been exposed in the news media to countless tales of the pragmatic and commonsensical nature of the Swedes.

Whatever level of legitimacy one is willing to grant to national characteristics —and their unreliability is notorious—it is true that the conflict in the tradition of Swedish poetry between the practical and mundane on the one hand and the mystical and rhetorical on the other is as old as it is real—even for the poetry of the last twenty-five years. One is probably justified in tracing its origin back to the eighteenth century, to the paradoxical fusion of enlightenment, rationalism and otherworldly speculation in the religious genius of Emanuel Swedenborg and of empirical scientific observation and restless seeking after the divine order in the taxonomic genius of Linnaeus. The highest attainments in Swedish poetry —by which I do not mean only what is recognized formally as poetry—have always in some sense been achieved through such a fusion, in the romantic poetry of E. J. Stagnelius and C. J. L. Almqvist, in Strindberg or Gustaf Fröding and, in our century, in the poetry of Vilhelm Ekelund, Birger Sjöberg, Gunnar Ekelöf and Erik Lindegren. One must not forget that, in the highest poetic triumphs of all these somehow broken or divided geniuses, there is something paradoxical and perhaps ultimately self-defeating which is very different from the unrelenting logic inherent in the intellectual development of Kierkegaard or Ibsen.

Accepting this fusion as the significant emblem of the genius of Swedish poetry—the mystic and the bureaucrat, the efficient engineers of images of transcendental dejection (internationally fashionable examples of figures cast in this mould are not uncommon: Dag Hammarskjöld and Ingmar Bergman come immediately to mind)—we must remember that the most prominent exponents of its tradition have been its victims rather than its exploiters. The relative poverty of this Swedish tradition merely exhibits an over-determined case; it is as much a result of contradictory impulses within itself, often causing irreparable damage to the cohesive powers of the mind or ego, as it is a reflection of the long economic indigence of the country. Hence also the frequent accusations levelled against Swedish literature (and art and film) for its indiscriminate predilections for gloom, madness and suicide. These result from the Swedish writer's incomplete projection onto a problematic scene of international modernism, and are not to any noticeable degree typical of his image seen from a Swedish viewpoint. There he appears rather to be defending sanity and 'realism' against the onslaught of a world gone mad. Hence also the often deplored suspiciousness in Sweden of those writers and artists who all too easily adapt themselves to the consumer demands of international art and culture. Quite misleadingly, this is often taken, at best, for insular provincialism, and, at worst, for plain old-fashioned envy (known idiomatically as the 'Royal Swedish disease'). It is no doubt with a genuine feeling of relief that the critic Lars Bäckström in a recent book[1] remarks on the 'lucky' fact that the Swedes at the moment 'do not yet have an *author* who is so exceedingly "multinationally" well-adapted and trivially brilliant as Ingmar Bergman appears to be in his films.' The mood of inward-looking self-sufficiency in this quotation may in its extreme wording be a fairly recent sign of disillusionment with the world cultural market, but it is still compatible with tendencies which have existed for a long time. In any case, it is a long cry from the avowed intentions of Strindberg to launch a 'conquest of Paris' and, from that vantage-point, of world literature.

II

'Modern'—'contemporary': the choice of terms is not exclusively a question of temporal sequence. Modern poetry and its derivative 'modernist' poetry have been with us since at least the latter half of the last century. In spite of the relatively venerable antiquity of modernism in its world-wide context, the phenomenon as a consolidated mode of experience or style is of fairly recent appearance in Sweden. Modernism on a broad basis came to that country, together with peace, prosperity, existentialism and the incipient cold war, just as 'heresy, hops and beer' to England in the old jingle, in 'the very same year'. This belated arrival of modernism is of the utmost importance for the formation of the Swedish poetry which we now regard as 'contemporary'. The 'modernist breakthrough'—in contrast to Brandes's 'modern breakthrough' in the 1870s and the 1880s—was an intensely compressed cultural event, taking place during a few years after World War II, in a period of auspicious publishing policies and economic optimism. Its coinciding with the social upheaval caused by the Social-Democratic reconstruction of Swedish society gave it a heroic aura and almost official sanction. Modernism became *the* language of poetry and literature: the ties with traditional forms and values were severed in a much more effective way than in countries where modernism had been a continuous process rather than an event.

This may account for some of the peculiar, and to some observers unattractive, aspects of contemporary Swedish poetry. As modernism proved to be not so much a mode of experience as simply a temporal event, soon exhausted and remaining only as a paradigm of bravery and moral fortitude, so it had to be replaced by strategies, often much more ephemeral, borrowed from outside the indigenous traditions. Shifting and fashionable attitudinizing, journalistic glibness and media-oriented trendiness have an undeniable presence in post-war Swedish poetry. 'Modernism' is always in danger of being replaced by 'modernity', and, as Paul de Man has shrewdly reminded us, it may be that literature (as a self-reflecting activity) and modernity are, in fact, incompatible concepts.[2]

III

Even a reader who has some previous acquaintance with Swedish poetry may have difficulty in establishing points of reference in the flux of ideas and events that constitute its more recent history. The literary scene has been extremely diversified but at the same time more vulnerable to external influences than would be the case in a less self-conscious cultural environment. (One noticeable characteristic of the Swedish writer in recent years has been his professionalism: the organizational practice of the Swedish Writers' Union *(Författarförbundet)* has served as a model for similar activities in other countries.)

During the three decades covered in the present anthology—which we believe to be the most comprehensive in the English language for many years—one can discern at least two important shifts in the intellectual awareness of the Swedish poet. The opening up of the world that occurred with the end of the war, gaining increasing impetus during the affluent fifties, ultimately resulted in a disillusion with the very forces which had created it. The more intimate contact with other—and in particular non-European—cultures, facilitated by the increased opportunities for travel and by the ever-growing flow of information in the sophisticated reporting of foreign affairs in Swedish newspapers (tendencies which existed elsewhere in the fifties and sixties, but gained importance earlier in Sweden) established the Swedish author in an often unenviable role as a self-appointed intermediary or spokesman for the Third World. The global conscience of a small and still comparatively isolated nation may easily incur the scorn of countries which have had longer-lasting relations with the more remote parts of the world and may lay it open to accusations of smugness and holier-than-thou moralizing. It cannot be denied that breast-beating and exhibitionist self-lacerations have played their part in some of these manifestations. On the other hand, it created the opportunity not only for some brilliant journalism and painstaking documentaries,[3] but also opened domains of poetry which could have been reached in no other way. Spanish, Latin-American and Francophone African poetry were introduced into Sweden and had an influence on Swedish poetry long before their impact was felt in America and England: the poems of Lasse Söderberg, Ingemar Leckius and, to some extent, Tomas Tranströmer bear witness to this.

The Vietnam war and what was known in Sweden as the FNL movement[4] had, I believe, a deeper impact on intellectual life in Sweden than in some countries more obviously concerned with the war itself. The development of an international political consciousness seemed at the time at least to be a mass movement. The supreme example of the appeal to political conscience is found in Göran Sonnevi's moving and subtle poetry which has had—considering its pure and uncompromising nature—an amazingly large following. His poem on the war in Vietnam[5] created almost overnight a demand for this kind of poetry which has hardly diminished even though the situation has altered. (It is interesting to note that his intricate poem on the use of napalm in American bombings of civilians in Vietnam, 'Will You Please Come In and Put on a Hat', which was in 1967 instantly understood by huge audiences mainly unfamiliar with modern poetry, now needs an explanatory note in order to be understood even by sophisticated readers. The clue to the poem is that napalm has the paradoxical property of burning more intensely when water is poured on it.) His latest book of poetry, *Det omöjliga* ('The Impossible', 1976) which runs to an impressive 431 pages, was chosen as Book of the Month and was printed in an inital edition of 10,000 copies.

The main formal influences of the militancy of the FNL-years are not, however, found in poetry as strongly as in the activities of small independent theatre groups like *Pistolteatern* and many others, and in the hybrids of traditional fighting songs and rock lyrics among various left-wing splinter groups. The major shift of emphasis came with the 1969–70 LKAB-strike.[6] Interest turned, almost imperceptibly at first, from global injustices to the equally real but more closely observed shortcomings of the capitalist system in the nominally socialist Sweden of today. Social, environmental and ecological issues in politics have for a long time been a matter of concern to many Swedes. The test-case for this second phase of political consciousness in Sweden came during the 1976 elections when the industrial use of nuclear power was one of the most important election issues. Although it apparently resulted in a victory for the abolitionists, the struggle still goes on. As a political movement this 'ecosophical' (as the latest jargon will have it) awareness is riddled with contradictions and internal antagonism: obviously, it is difficult to reconcile the demands for devolution of environmentally detrimental energy sources with equally legitimate demands for full employment.

If this new awareness still seems to be struggling with its political persona, it has certainly proved to be very fertile in poetry. Göran Sonnevi again provided what seems to be the *locus classicus* of the political struggle against nuclear power in his poem 'A mother stands in front . . .'. The more broadly 'ecosophical' issues are found especially in Gösta Friberg's thoughtful and beautifully modulated poetry, for example in the global and interplanetary scenery of 'The Growing'. It is a tendency which is at present fast gaining in importance.

IV

Every anthologist knows how useless it is to hope that explanations or apologies will save him from accusations of unforgiveable omissions. The only course seems to be boldly to assert one's freedom of choice.

Many diverse considerations have influenced the selection of poets for this volume. No poets of the older generation have been included even though their writing has been in the process of fertile development during the period covered. We decided to limit our choice mainly to poets aged under fifty, although one or two might have passed that age by the time this book appears (and one had reached it just before her tragic death). In other cases, we felt that poets who would have been a natural choice were already adequately translated into English: for example, Tomas Tranströmer, Östen Sjöstrand, Lars Gustafsson and Gunnar Harding have each had at least one book-length collection of their work published in translation.[7] Lars Forssell would, of course, be worthy of a much fuller introduction, but his *oeuvre* is now so extensive and versatile that only a volume would suffice. The same applies to Sandro Key-Åberg whose highly original and inventive style may raise insurmountable difficulties for the translator.

Other arguments have been decisive in other cases. Some poets, or groups of poets, we just did not like or found wanting in poetic weight. This goes for most of the 'new simplicity' or 'minimalism' of the early sixties, and for some of the more breezily rhetorical of the militant political poetry of recent years, be it motivated by the class struggle or the women's movement. It also applies to some cloyingly 'confessional' poets of the middle generation. We would have liked to include more of the best women poets (there are many writing in Swedish) and some of the Swedish-language poets of Finland who are now, as they have been traditionally, in the forefront of poetic creativity. Considerations of space and balance have tied our hands here. We were unable to give any examples of 'concrete' poetry, which has played a very important part in Sweden (where in fact the term originated, invented by the late Öyvind Fahlström). At least one truly original poet among the 'concretists', Bengt

Emil Johnsson, would have been a self-evident choice, had we not felt that his work would disrupt the unity of this volume. We have also had to leave out some very young poets, be they neo-formalists like Jesper Svenbro or neo-rhetorical romantics like Bruno K. Öijer.

Finally, the selection can be accused of a certain provincial (and in this case most persistently Southern) bias. Of the fifteen poets represented here, eight have their origins or are at present living in the south of Sweden. This is no doubt partly due to the inveterate regional consanguinity of one of the translators, but also, it is more seriously a deliberate attempt to get away from the more drearily fashionable shenanigans that so often set their stamp on the literary life of the capital. Different selections could certainly be made with equal conviction taking other parts of Sweden (or Finland) as a vantage point.

V

In short, this anthology does not lay claims to strict objectivity. But nor is it a random choice of what the translators happen to like at the moment. The emphasis has been on the contemporary scene, on what seems fertile today. No poet or poems have been included because he or they were deemed to be representative of some trend or tendency; on the other hand, obviously our evaluation of individual poets or poems may vary quite considerably. Our guide-lines have been: first, poetic excellence as we see it and, secondly, translatability. One often encounters in anthologies of this type poems which are so enmeshed in their original culture, so full of references to local traditions and history, that they have to be glossed and explicated to extinction. We have deliberately avoided such poems. We think that the apparent involvement with traditional roots in, for example, the long poems by Sonja Åkesson or Tomas Tranströmer is of such a universal nature that the poems transcend what is merely local or historical. Similarly, in the longish poem by Göran Palm which refers to a specifically Swedish cultural scene, the satirical intent behind the delightfully generalized inanities carries such conviction that anybody with some experience of the more sublime idiocies of our Western culture must feel instantly at home.

An explanation may be needed for the arrangement of the anthology. The ten poets who make up the main part of the volume have all been carefully chosen so as to be presented at some length. In the introductory section 'Do you know the country?' we brought together poems on the whole by slightly older poets not represented in the second part of the anthology, to illustrate certain attitudes to Sweden or to local or personal history seen from a perspective which is in one way or another characteristic of recent Swedish poetry. These poems cannot be taken as being in themselves representative of their authors' rich and variegated work. They are intended rather as visiting cards announcing the poets' presence at a certain time and scene which is important to the general picture. The moral dilemma of Sweden's relation to the world is placed in the poem by Forssell squarely in the equivocal fact that Swedish peace and prosperity depends on arms sales and thus on war and carnage. This points in a decisive way to a key, a mood, in which much of the best subsequent poetry is played. The poem by Tranströmer which concludes this section is indicative of a rival mood: that of intense searching in the personal and local history which he invokes. It seems to me that between them these two poems encompass the whole scale of experience in which Swedish poetry has been moving in the last twenty years. As a supplement we have the full acceptance of a Swedish background in the attractively straightforward 'confessional' poem of Sonja Åkesson and its negation, the absence of any recognizable Swedish voice or experience (its language apart) in Söderberg's poem which is fully assimilated into its Spanish theme.

The poets in the main anthology section all are, I believe, in various ways and to various degrees, involved in the self-reflectiveness of poetry: they are all endeavouring to come to terms with specific problems or situations created by their relation to the tradition of Swedish poetry and to Swedish culture in general. This seems to me more valuable than the ethnic quaintness that is often sought in poetry translated from a foreign language. In their acceptance of the antinomies of the predicament of being 'modern', they are trying to eschew mere 'modernity', the bland simulacra of fashion.

This is perhaps what in the last analysis brings these disparate poets together. There is an enormous difference between the taut, sparse, firmly articulated poetry of Majken Johansson—to my mind the strongest and most original woman poet writing in Swedish after Edith Södergran—and the steady flow of images in the brilliantly expansive poetry of Lars Norén. But they are united in the despair which they articulate, a despair which can be alleviated only by the poetry itself or, in the case of Majken Johansson, by religion which to her seems to be a pristine form of poetry. (She has been active for twenty years as a Salvation Army officer.) Similarly, the open, flexible assimilation of experience in Jan Östergren's poetry could not be less like the discursive mythopolitical musings of Tobias Berggren. Yet both question not only their material but the very forms in which their experience is shaped. In the essay previously referred to, Heidegger ascribed this knowledge to the 'venturesome' poets he found valid for destitute times: 'The mark of these poets is that to them the nature of poetry becomes worthy of questioning, because they are poetically on the track of that which, for them, is what must be said'.[8] We hope that the urgency of these poems will be heard clearly through the masks of our translation.

Göran Printz-Påhlson
Cambridge, 1978

Notes

1 *Kulturarbete—kritik 68–77* (Stockholm, 1978), p.28.
2 *Blindness and Insight—Essays on the Rhetoric of Contemporary Criticism* (New York, 1971).
3 The names that come to mind are Per Wästberg, Sven Lindkvist, Sara Lidman. See Janet Mawby, 'Writers and Politics' in *Modern Scandinavia* (London, 1977).
4 The identification with the Vietnamese National Liberation Front was the easier as the derogatory and contemptuous term 'Vietcong' was avoided by Swedish news media.
5 Not included in this volume. Several translations into English exist. See e.g. that by Robin Fulton, *Lines Review* no. 35, December 1970.
6 The strike of the miners and workers of the Luossavaara-Kirunavaara Company highlighted unsuspected hardships and resentments and dispelled the unrealistic notions of ideal industrial relations in Sweden, entertained both abroad and at home.
7 Östen Sjöstrand, *The Hidden Music. Selected Poems* translated by Robin Fulton, Oleander Press (Cambridge and New York, 1975); Lars Gustafsson, *Selected Poems* translated by Robin Fulton, New Rivers Press (New York, 1972); Gunnar Harding, *They Killed Sitting Bull and other Poems* translated by Robin Fulton, London Magazine Editions (London, 1973). Of the many translations of Tomas Tranströmer the most important are *Windows and Stones: Selected Poems* translated by May Swenson and Leif Sjöberg, University of Pittsburgh Press (Pittsburgh, 1972); *Night Vision* translated by Robert Bly, London Magazine Editions (London, 1972); *Selected Poems* (with Paavo Haavikko) translated by Robin Fulton, Penguin Books (Harmondsworth, 1975) and *Baltics*, translated by Samuel Charters, Oyez Press (Berkeley, 1975). See further the special issue of *Ironwood* (13) on Tranströmer (Tucson, 1979).
8 Martin Heidegger, *Poetry, Language, Thought*, translated by Albert Hofstadter (New York, 1975), p.141.

Note

Göran Printz-Påhlson gives me more credit for these translations and for the shape of this volume than I deserve. When our collaboration began I knew no Swedish at all and very little about contemporary Swedish poetry. Clearly, the choices of texts had to be entirely his. I did, however, refuse to continue working on a couple of poems he chose (because I so disliked them!) and am proud to have insisted all along on the inclusion of his own fine work with that of his contemporaries. These acts of censorship and persuasion constitute the extent of my editorial contribution to this book.

We began all of our translations huddled together over the Swedish text and a blank piece of paper; I was never given the cribs or trots or drafts in prose which seem to be customary in collaborative translation to 'work up' into an English poem. We worked together on each poem from scratch, taking it a word, a phrase, a line at a time. I think we may have hit upon solutions to various problems by working in this manner that we would have never discovered had we been passing drafts back and forth (and we certainly grew used to sharing some long silences). For some of the best translations here I functioned only as amanuensis and typist. I suggested nothing and changed nothing as Gösta Friberg's 'Nobody' appeared in Printz-Påhlson's English before us. Some of the Sonnevi poems (though by no means all) also went easily and immediately into English with no modifications offered along the way by the junior partner; so did some of Lars Norén and some of Peter Ortman; so did Sonja Åkesson's 'A Letter'. In the case of other poems—Friberg's 'The Growing', for example—Printz-Påhlson and I had to struggle with the text and with each other for days. I must bear most of the responsibility for occasional problematic liberties taken with some texts. I am conscious in general of a tendency to use an overly insistent iambic rhythm to solve (or bulldoze) metrical problems. I am guilty now and then of radical re-lineation. Once or twice I have been obstinately gratuitous (Norén's burning cattle really only have 'shaven' and not exactly 'tonsured' skulls; Forssell's line which in fact means 'bread means death' ends up 'stealth means wealth' because I stubbornly insisted on retaining a full rhyme and didn't like 'bread means dead'). And so on. The problems are familiar to all translators and to nearly all readers of translation.

I want to thank Clare Hall, Cambridge for the Visiting Fellowship that I held during the academic year 1976–77 which enabled me to collaborate with Göran Printz-Påhlson on this project at the same time as I was completing work of a wholly different kind. In nearly ideal circumstances, and with an endless supply of hot coffee, Printz-Påhlson and I were able to work steadily, without interruption of any kind, on the translations that make up this book. We were able to enjoy those long and productive silences in silence.

John Matthias
University of Notre Dame
March, 1979

Part I: Do You Know The Country?

LARS FORSSELL

Sweden in the Summer

> *Kennst Du das Land wo die Kanonen blühen?*
> —Kästner

Do you know the country where the cannon blooms
And spreads its pollen all across the earth?
Fertilizes wars to blossom scabs on wounds,
Bleeding flower cups across the earth,
Poppies like grenades?
Do you know that country? Do you know that country?
Do you know the country where the cannon blooms?

In fact it's called Sweden, on a kind of lake,
A naked image on the surface of the water
Or in a camera lens. Often she boasts
Of her voluptuous figure
And of her social welfare
Paid for by cultivating cannons
Made in Bofors where the summer breeze
Spreads nefarious pollen on the earth . . .
The welfare of the country is nefarious,
Made of the putrescence from the cannons
At the shores of Bofors looming red
In sunset all across the earth.
Such is the motto of Sweden in a heat wave
That stealth means wealth.

Do you know the country where the cartridge blooms?
And not the squires, like partridges,
Who once drove farmers off to work with walking sticks—
I mean cartridges for guns
With which in other countries
Other men kill men
Far beyond the lake slick with herring shoals
In which Sweden gazes at herself contentedly
Far, far from the sound of harps

From all their golden strings tumbling down the cliffs
Of Bofors... Do you know that country?

So far far away that reports are never heard
By those who lie voluptuously sprawling
On the beaches of the lake or have their
Photos in *Expressen*
With their heavy virgin breasts
In the summer, when according to tradition
Warlords seized the chance
And the wars competitively bloomed...

Do you know the country where the cannon blooms?
Do you know that country? Do you know that country?
It's called Sweden, and it lies by Bofors
Basking in the sun
While Swedish steel bites abroad
Leaving teeth of bullets
In the skin of other men...

The Swedish skin is being bitten thigh and bum
By mosquitoes and the sun.
A stranger howls running bent with pain and fright
While the Swedish sun is burning bright.
Your glowing shrapnel sun
Warrants mine.
Do you know the country where the cannon blooms?
Do you know the country where the cartridge blooms?
Do you know that country? Do you know that country?
It's called Sweden.

Bofors: Swedish armaments factory, world-renowned for its anti-aircraft weaponry, 'the Bofors gun'.

Expressen: a leading Swedish evening tabloid.

LASSE SÖDERBERG

The Capital of Fear

1

The sun and the leather, the well and the saint.
The red city closes around its empty halls.
The noon carries its wound through the streets.

I remember how the postcards shrivelled up.
How the tourist was kept hanging in the dawn.
How the cloud ceased to function.

And the children, how can I forget them.
The day slants steeply down into my skull.
Wind carries the thin children through the trees.

2

The dead children in the river Tajo,
Swaddled in the sheets of the water,
The dead children in the river Tajo.

Silently they speak to the fishes, silently
They inhabit the mud of the river bed. I hear them murmur,
More beautiful than grass, in coffins of glass.

The dead children with earthen eyes,
With silent earthen eyes in the river Tajo:
Theatre of hunger under a freezing sun.

3

At last they arrive in the Capital of Fear
Which crumbles high on its rock above the river.
Behind their pale foreheads still snow falls.

And the foam crowns them, they travel in light
Far away from any human shores,
They cultivate their wonder, rest in a murmur of paper.

There is a death inside them made of paper,
A water death in the buzzing infinite room
Beneath the murmur and the sun and the mother's cry.

4

To recover the red city in the cloud,
Sun and the leather, saint and the well: sacred images
In too many processions, too many cathedrals.

Night raises its ladder into a heavenly mist,
To the dawn and its rocking pavilions,
To a world of crumbling stone, a world of paper.

Night, silent around me, frail
High above the river. The river: a final gurgling
At the bottom of Toledo.

GÖRAN PALM

On This Earth

It was morning in my room, in our country, on this earth
It was raining, I felt uncommonly spry
And in the furthest corner of the space bus we saw Bunny Cinnamon, and
    he looked as if he was going to be sick because he had gorged himself
    on a whole bag of Clandies, that sounds funny, do you know Olle
    what Clandies are?—a special kind of sweet that only Bun
Exhaustion set in
Yeah yeah yeah
What's happening in the world, what do they say about *me*?
ENTIRE POPULATION OF CITY MADE HOMELESS AFTER QUAKE
Calmly and with concentration I began to write an article
All the relations were cowering in the cupboard
Bloody typewriter
While I was eating it suddenly came to me just how logical positivism
    really hangs together
Yes that must be it, a brilliant idea
The Beatles were ringing in my ears, yeah yeah
What's that now?
TAKE ANYTHING YOU LIKE AND COMPARE IT WITH PASCAL
I felt guilty about something that happened in 1947
Why didn't the post arrive?
Positivism?
Hello, is that Hugo, long time no see. No, you don't disturb me at all.
    What? That sounds great. Thursday then? Look here, a terrific idea!
    Yes, of course, I'd love to
No idea
A man came walking by with sheets
IN SWEDEN WE LEAD A MUCH TOO SHELTERED LIFE
A minibus goes racing through the hallway
Why don't I get anything done
The sun came out
What's that thing coming towards me? TAKE IT AWAY
No letters, only advertisements and bills
Fine white dust is floating over the floor
Yesterday we went to a party

We danced and laughed ourselves silly
HANS ALFREDSON, THE COMEDIAN, IS TERRIFIC
What good people they all were, we could talk about nuclear war without anyone getting aggressive
At the gate my father stood
I bought some aspirins
THIS CAN'T POSSIBLY GO ON ANY LONGER
A table fell over when they were dancing, then they became insufferable
Dusk fell
Look, a kite in the sky
Dusk fell
There are seconds and minutes which present themselves with such extravagance that you feel exiled from history and the world, and there is nothing you can depend on because *everything* is now: your entire expelled power is spent on whispering yourself into, in imploring yourself into, my love, my love, what's on T.V.?
The investiture of a new pope
TAKE IT AWAY
We were taking measurements for curtains
With softly raised hands we were taking measurements for curtains
WHAT IS IT ALL ABOUT FOR CHRIST'S SAKE
The darkness gently insinuated itself among the pleats
Then there was a hitch
Bloody Hell The Damn Bloody Curtains!
My name is Councillor Frisk, do I disturb your dinner?
The dust settled
'B' INTERNATIONAL: SWEDEN–NORWAY: 0–0
Children were singing in the basement
I was thinking of death
And Bob's your uncle
We procrastinated
De Gaulle was giving a speech, Vive la France
WITH A LOVE LIKE THAT/YOU KNOW YOU SHOULD BE GLA-AA-AAD
The article was finished
Hungry people queueing outside the kitchen
The point is to choose an attitude to life which is congenial
Desolate hours, everyone in his room
How about going on a bender? taking a walk? having a fight?

Arms hanging loose from the chairs
But when you pass through Saigon for the last time at dawn, a Saigon
    where in spite of everything life seems to be getting back to normal,
    you cannot suppress the thought that whichever side in the long run
Everything was reinforced concrete
Suddenly I arose with a miraculously simple heart
Something had become important
Evening was restored by grace
I was no longer alone in my room, I wrote and wrote
O that life can be so rich
The sky and the stars belong to everyone
ALWAYS KEEP JESUS IN YOUR THOUGHTS
A crowd of hungry people
What was the thing I was never going to forget?
The man who lives upstairs fell over
A saw inside which cuts through the skin, NO
Then we tumbled each other onto our bed
I was thinking of my neighbour's wife
Such fun
On the 474th lap a squalid spacecraft passed
It was night, yeah yeah
Pajamas and paralysis
Shall we not, now at the end of day, forget all small and paltry things and
    give thanks, from the depths of our hearts, for the day which has
    gone by? Was it not full of riches, did we not receive it as a gift from
    above? It received us
Sleep tight
A window banging
The fork to the left and the knife to the right
What are we really doing
On this earth

SONJA ÅKESSON

A Letter

Hasse!
Hans Evert!
Do you remember me?

I was not your first girl friend
of course
but you were my first boy friend.

You rode your bike all the time, a Rambler,
and wore your hat on the back of your head
and I got to ride on the handlebars in my red cloak
and sometimes on the back.

One night we rode into the ditch.

And those songs you sang.
Even then they were old:
*Home to my girl
sooner or later
I'll return
home to my girl
home to my girl*

I can just hear your voice:
saffron and cinnamon and a few mustard seeds
and also you slurred all your notes.

Your sister was fat and called Jenny.

When we started you were seventeen and I—
I don't dare to tell.
You could have gone to jail.

You always had a suntan.

Then the war broke out.

Do you remember the cottage on the lake
with the chickens and the cat and the birch trees?

Think if we were living there now.

I'd have probably had umpteen children
who washed their hands and faces
in a bucket
before they went to Sunday school.

Your fat sister Jenny
would have been my sister-in-law.

But I wouldn't have known my mother-in-law.
She had been shot by your father
who then cut his own throat
with a razor blade.

You showed me pictures of them once.

Sometimes you were a little drunk.
Then you had jasmine twigs
or pear blossoms
on your handlebars.

Once you did it
with another girl.

When your father went berserk you hid in a cupboard.
He was going to shoot you children too.

Every night I lied.
I had never told a fib before.

When I lied I pretended
that it wasn't me.

I pretended it was a dream.

I pretended that it wasn't even me
who dreamed.

My mother smelled faintly of apples.
Her hair had fallen down.
She wept
and I wept too in spasms

even though it was nothing but a dream,
even though it wasn't even me.

Every day was one long dream.

One night mother sat there in her coat and hat.

Think if they had done it,
I mean if they had sent me away.
Imagine—me! who used to cry so hard for mother
when I had spent a week at cousin Ruth's.

You were kind to children.
No, I'm not being sarcastic.
I was not a child.

You were kind to the farmer's children.
You were kind to the old help.
They said you were kind to the farmer's kids
and to the old woman.

On the wind I send you this greeting
To my father and mother and girl.
On the wind I send it on fleeting
To my father and mother and girl.

When you sang your Adam's apple bobbed.

Your father had been disabled for a long time.
Maybe after some accident.

Your mother looked so pretty in the picture.

Then the war came,
and I wasn't the girl friend
of anybody in particular
for several years.

For several years I never lied.

I heard you became a Pentecostal
and married later on, into some money
and a farm, another Pentecostal.

I met you once.

You asked God to forgive you, you said.
I thought that sounded silly.
I knew you wanted me.

How old can you possibly be now?
45?

Are you still saved?
Do you think your father is in Hell?

Do you still smell of horses?

But I'm sure you own a tractor.

TOMAS TRANSTRÖMER

Baltic Seas III

In a dim corner of the Gotland church, colour of mild mold
there is a christening font of sandstone—12th century—the stonemason's name
still there, glowing
like a row of teeth in a mass grave:
                         HEGWALDR
                                the name remains.
     And his pictures
here and on the sides of other crocks, swarms of people, shapes emerging from the stone.
The nuclei of goodness and evil in their eyes are bursting there.
Herod at the table: the cock in the serving dish flies up and crows
     Christus natus est—the waiter was executed—
close by the child is born, under clusters of faces dignified and helpless like young monkeys.
And the fleeing footfalls of the pious
echoing across the gaping dragonscaled sewers.
(The images stronger in memory than when directly observed, stronger
when the font turns in the slow rumbling roundabout of memory.)
Nowhere shelter. Everywhere risk.
As it was. As it is.
Only inside is there peace, in the water of the font which nobody sees,
but on the outer sides the struggle goes on.
And peace may come drip by drip, perhaps at night
when we are unaware,
or as when one is on drips in a hospital ward.

Men, beasts, ornaments.
There is no landscape. Ornaments.

Mr B*** my fellow-tourist, amiable, exiled,
released from Robben Island, says:
'I envy you. I feel nothing for nature.
But *people in a landscape*, that tells me something.'

Here are people in a landscape.
A photograph from 1865. A steam-launch anchored at the quay
    in the inlet.
Five figures. A lady in light crinoline, like a bell, like a flower.
The men look like extras in a rustic play.
All of them are handsome, hesitating on the verge of fading out.
They disembark for a little while. They fade out entirely.
The steam-launch is an obsolete model—
high funnel, sun tent, narrow hull—
it is utterly alien, a UFO which has landed.
Everything else in the photograph is shockingly real:
the ripples on the water,
the other shore—
I can rub my hand across the rugged rocks,
I can hear the whispering of the wind in the spruce trees.
It is near. It is
today.
The waves are contemporary.

Now, a hundred years later. The waves come from *no man's water*
and pound against the rocks.
I walk along the shore. It isn't as it used to be to walk along the shore.
One has to yearn for so much, speak to many people at once, live with
    such thin walls.
Every object has got a new shadow behind the ordinary shadow
and you hear it dragging along even when it is entirely dark.

It is night.

The strategic planetarium turns. The lenses stare into darkness.
The nocturnal sky is full of numbers, and they are being fed
into a flashing box,
a piece of furniture
which contains the energy of a swarm of locusts eating acres of the crops of
    Somalia in half an hour.

I don't know if we are at the beginning or at the terminal stage.

Recapitulation cannot be made, recapitulation is impossible.

Recapitulation is the mandrake root—
(*vide* the Dictionary of Superstitions:
                              MANDRAKE
                                                    magical herb
which let out such a terrifying scream when it was pulled out of the
    ground
that one would fall down dead. The dog had to do it . . .)

Robben Island: Prison island outside the coast of South Africa, where many of the opponents of apartheid are being detained.

Part II: Anthology

INGEMAR LECKIUS

On Another Planet

He had always wanted to live in a waterfall. Why? To conquer the fear of death, he said.

But he lived on another planet where there were no waterfalls. Everything was hard and immovable.

He lived in a fence. A fence of gold, admittedly, but still—

He died of fear, almost immediately.

Family Life

I

During the long rainy winter nights when the wind is howling outside, my wife and I often play cards. We play in complete silence and we play with our bodies as stakes.

After half an hour or so, I consider my losses to have been sufficient. I get up from the table saying calmly: 'Let's stop playing now. I have nothing more I can lose. I have lost the whole outside of my body.' The inside of my body I am eager to keep.

But my wife will never let it go at that. Threateningly, she forces me to continue the game. And we never stop playing until I have lost my whole body. Only my diseases—the headache, the cold, and all my fevers—remain on my side of the table.

Such evenings are indeed pretty miserable.

II

For four years now I have been busy building a rocking chair. That was in order to get even with my wife who had been building a bed without a back. Now it was my turn to build a rocking chair.

A rocking chair without a seat.

A rocking chair for dreamers.

I can't understand how it happened, but I was only able to make the seat. And what could be done with that? It was not supposed to be there at all.

But in the meantime my wife had managed to build a dredging machine which filled the whole house and forced me out into the street.

At the moment I'm making a steam engine. When it is finished I'll go away. But so far I have only managed to make lots of steam, which is a bloody damn nuisance to look after.

III

My eyesight suddenly started to fail.

My wife gave me an old spyglass without any lenses. 'Now let's play hide-and-seek,' she said. And then she vanished forever.

And I, I am completely powerless. I am compelled to run around with this ancient telescope.

Before, I could spot a tiger from several yards away. But now I never find it.

I just go on and on in the semi-darkness.

Magister Caput

Look, the trespasser comes—
with a beard like a hurricane, with a black cloak.
He hurls himself into the throng like a poltergeist.

We disperse like children.
We run breathlessly towards the horizon.
But he quickly overtakes us with his bat-like wings.
 Nightly operations—
Already darkness arises inside us.
And the bubble breaks out of the carpenter's level.
The trespasser, cruel and fawning, has come to stay.

Look at the prompter, our peer! The animal trainer!
He changes our faces to slates where he writes the word ENTRÉE.
He inveigles himself, he caresses our weakness.
He invades us further and further, playing the organ of shadows.

Ingemar Leckius

Now he is all at once far ahead of us.
O labyrinth of terror—

He turns around, *magister caput*.
Like a customs official he confiscates our identity.
We turn wholly into one murmuring sound.
He invades us more deeply than we have ever been ourselves.
   Nightly opera—
We follow the trespasser; we ourselves shall build his throne.

But at the very centre silence waits.
Surprised, we see our sovereign stagger and fall.

Silence. Night.
Extras in the desert. Who will find us here again?

Paul Klee

I

With the lever of dreams
he lifts the rock of night.
A spade among the stars
makes his destiny glow.

II

A boy climbs the gangway ladder of song.
See his indomitable banners in the wind!

He crawls to the end of the sea shell.
A love call rises from the Cambrian deserts.
He steps into an ancient oak tree
and recovers his own image there.

The murmuring palaces of the sea
he opens with a key of salt.

III

The subterranean flowers
blossom at the command of the story teller
but give scent only at the child's request.

IV

The painter reshapes geometry.
An incision in the skin of night.

He traverses with a smile
the caravan of unending winters.

He finds a new equilibrium.
Wonder lives in both his eyes.

He summons the doves
and dresses in their velvet.

While the pyramids are whispering
about their secret windows.

V

He offers her everything blue.
They lie on the beach of infinity.
Their intimate friend is ceramics.

They recognize each other's heartbeats
and the telegrams of wave crests.

VI

Two hearts beat together.
Two parallel lines meet.

Ingemar Leckius

Mirobolus Makadam & Co.

(Jean Dubuffet)

I am whole and hot
Lava flows out of my eyes
I'm not much moved to look out

I stick my tongue out at darkness
which swallows it

I have no teeth
But I have pebbles
to whistle with

I am so ugly I lose my ears
I laugh so much that I vanish

I am implacable
On my wailing belly everyone pounds
                              in vain

Speakers in Tongues

(Arshile Gorky)

They sink
Their youth is a trap
They rise
They swirl in the wind like petals

They carry each other
Their voices swing on trapezes
They are restrained

> A rope from arm to arm
> They grow old
>
> Only the words dream: O to be hurled suddenly out of
> the mouth hanging like a universal joint!

Metaphysics

I

Inaccessible fire!
Facing perfect beauty
I am gripped by rage
and I want to destroy ...
Is that the reason why the diamond
is so hard?

II

In the fabulous silence
before birdsong breaks at dawn
I listen to my pulse
as if to a message in some unknown code.
      From where? From where ...

To a Zen Monk

In the hanging temple
man can neither be deposed
nor crowned. I cannot bear
the immutable smile
under the firmament, Tao's
      brilliant emptiness.

Ingemar Leckius

I prefer the rain storm
in the night of time, the half-dissolved
face in Gethsemane. There is
a transformation which is completed
                in the darkness of the earth.

The Voyeurs of Suffering

We watch the man of hunger on T.V. He can't see us.
His eyes have lost themselves in blackened skies.

The charitable appeals multiply! But we sink
deeper into our armchairs, our diving bells of compassion.

Time has stopped for him out there, and for us
who are nailed to our peepholes of Hell.

In the Desert the Wild Sheep Roam
      to Frantz Fanon

They silently accept our old blankets,
our surplus fodder, our grants.

They refuse to be promoted honorary beings.
Imperceptibly an earthquake shakes the world.

They shed the yoke of our compassion.
Their eye slits look like gun muzzles.

It doesn't help confessing our guilt,
it doesn't help sweating out our whiteness.

Strategy grows in their muscles.
Knives are honed in their bowels.

We who have always turned the others' cheeks,
how can we escape the wrath that comes?

Scintilla Animae

To have a vision is to overtake that which does not move.

There are words which burn, which burn forever, but which never burn to ash.

*

The one who ceases to wait buries himself.
But there is also a waiting which is a catapult! A sinking which is like a leap!
The sand is blowing. I follow the Absent One close at heel. Silence is a compass.

Even the mole crawls toward a horizon

There are thousands of roads which lead nowhere, or just one road in the darkness. A road which is naked, which is waiting to be dressed in footsteps.
With my mouth pressed to the ground I hear the stones call out.

O blood which runs through the body and never finds its way back to the heart...

*

I turn inwards and am pulled away from my vision.
And in this utter darkness, which is no longer mine, I hear somebody say:
Believe in the spark!

MAJKEN JOHANSSON

Little Dialectic for Poets

The sun is at its height, so high.
The picture forces its frame,
everything creaks in its joints . . .

and your hands and feet
refuse to do only what hands and feet
can do.—
But your tongue wanted only to speak,
whereafter you went to everyone and said:
I am a poet, here is my axe and spade!
But loneliness, O Procrustes, is counted in years, not days.

And your friends have theirs,
the whole world has its gods and always someone.
Only you, only that you
can do nothing before you stop
doing one thing
                    or another.

A House of Gertrude Stein

This is a place where you adopt children
as if you would purchase silk cushions,
a place where you have a lean housemaid
in sullen Flemish national dress.
It is a place where you find large white women,
helpless and intelligent and softly indifferent.

It is a place in the south, with plenty of food
and almost no money
a place where you go mad in the spring,
crazy and dangerous to all except for the
green soft silk cushions purchased
like adopted children.

Gertrude Stein Again

Flat limp sentimentality
heating centre
impotence.
And paracitation, like para-
            phrases
            llels (abundant)
        and the noia
ever parading.

Later deworming, depoisoning,
end to end.
Thereafter blind, paraplegic,
deaf and dumb but in good health. All the heartbeats.
Bullying.

I didn't mean that at all.
Only a small misfortune, raised to the level
of accident, a misfortune which accidentally
is epidemic and hereditary.

Not least in the world of fiction.

René Descartes

And I looked apart between the soul and body
so deeply, that there grew loneliness. So deeply
that there grew loneliness more keen.

A soul, and a body,
and Me pinched
in between.
Once in a while you have to choke with laughter, like when
Descartes came trotting up with *glandula pinealis* in his hand.
And everything else that is foolish,
and everything else than good.

Majken Johansson

The orderly creature taught me
the names of heaven and hell. (Such was also
the fall of Socrates.)

And because of that
it is not an attempt to be witty
when all the time I speak with cloven tongue

and look the happier, the more I tremble.

Descartes believed that he had found the residence of the human soul in the pituitary gland *(glandula pinealis)*.

Excursion

Here is a forest full of high conclusions,
straight, white trees, with sap drained long ago.
The greenery
         is strictly, strictly for the birds.

Come and build in this our forest,
come and dare to build!
You flee? with luncheon baskets slung across your backs!
O No, and now the hunt begins. Ants cross your path,
a pack of worms surrounds you.
Somebody blows *allstot*.
         Then it all died.

There is Aristotle, an indifferent form among the trees
measuring their golden means. Dusk falls
and ants and worms and birds
have left the forest, last of all.
Moon, take cover! now the forester arrives
to mark.

A Meditation

1

Apples are good for the teeth, they keep them apart.
Apples aren't any good for the teeth, they soften them up.
—hear here what we must ask ourselves!
The free will of teeth, to stop chewing,
the ripeness of apples, its part in the origin and end of the species
—we don't abandon to its fate
what we think is fate itself.
Except for the toothless
this is moral science and philosophy.

2

Their happy category:
shrunken, gaping, wheezing like wind in a windpipe
before the origin of everything
after the end of everything
they come and go.
A better mouth than ours
makes their plea.

3

Surely life is good for us, it keeps us apart.
Life is unhappy for us, it divides us
from our dead. There it is:
what we must continue or cease
to chew or spit out.

To the Forbears

1

Then I was hanging as among the carefully
ordered ropes of change-ringing—
up, down, up—

Majken Johansson

the bells raining and the words singing and chiming
down on my back when I slowly arose.

I groped across the pictures of their faces,
the bedclothes which lacerated me and carried me
when still I had not learned to lie or lay
or rise or move without at once
dissolving into a thousand semaphores
—still I feel the change-rung pain of it.

Yet in the middle of eternity
I sprawled now long ago.
Complaining:
'Death does not come, although I wish it.
The other day I saw her, she was white and black.
She did not even fondle me.'

2

Now I am not much younger,
do not know about time . . .
As when falling and falling down
through the floors.
Nothing in them is chiming, no bellwords.
There the seconds live domiciled in wood,
and are neither visible nor nomads.

The Demons

These pitiful demons, sprouting here
in my flower pots. There they are
fingers locked in tug-of-war.
Some are hanging flushed with exertion
upside down from my windowsill.

Nor is it any better
under my pillow.

There sleeps Daimon with an open mouth,
dreaming that the prison uniform of night
is a toga. How innocence takes pains!

Morning is to be distributed
between arms and legs, head and neck.
Morning is to be distributed
between jacket and trousers, heart and knife.
Morning is to be dedicated
to the memory of the demons.

Elegy at a Grave

In such a numbness dwells the sun
that spring itself is shedding leaves,
the summer doesn't even reach to autumn.
Space is lowered
pale and cold inside the grave.
The spade has done its spadework.

Without space, what is breath?
Something beats, calls itself
with desperate motions
heart.
Heart! To be alive!

*

Pardon me but once again: *heart*.
Pardon me, spade, but I really do mean
heart.
Never a line which is not true.
Already now I do not dare.

And then it falls—
irony with a stolid: *ha!*
Splendid rhythm with a wingtorn: *kra*.

Majken Johansson

The pregnant pause, the looming end, all the glow-worms
in other words, and yet more
other words and others' words—well . . .

*

You have to?
You have to start playing in the midst of everything
with scissors and rulers.
However I toss
sorrow is
not half as pale as you.

*

'And the last thing I said was . . . '
'And the last thing you said was . . . '
Nothing above the ground, is it?
said the spade.

*

For this life
is the afterlife.
Wait: eternity waits
in eternity.

*

'Give us flesh on the bones!'
What kind of flesh?
Consider the dead,
they do not complain.

Staircase

A Sunday morning in autumn
the sun shines down on Nybroplan
brilliantly into my eyes.
Still in the staircases of memory
anxiety clings to hundreds
of old and empty whisky bottles.
Two men at Slussen busy themselves
emptying one more.
'Why are you so desolate, my soul,
and anxious inside me?'

In the uniform of the Salvation Army
I walk quickly to the south
eager to worship
in one of many places
the One who said
to a woman, crippled for eighteen years:
you are free.

'And presently she straightened up
and praised the Lord.'

Nostalgic Letter to G.P.-P.

The ontological proof
we once put in the mail box of the newspaper. Now
we have to struggle against documentaries.
How
can you break out of reality
and into 'the elastic picture'
when the soft erasers of Robbe-Grillet
every day
harden to lines of chalk
across the blackboard?
They have the shape of Vs,
but capital ones, as in Vietnam.

Majken Johansson

Otherwise,
we buy some food every day; read, I suppose.
I miss you in your black Cambridge garb.
The colour
suits us all, as you should know.

GÖRAN PRINTZ-PÅHLSON

Broendal

Raining no longer. (Water like a mirror)
The words are all bright in your mouth.
White light on the wet pavement. Language a mirror
Or another way of breathing outside your mouth?

We are speaking and the words are all white.
The wind speaks to the rain and the rain to the sea
And the wind is blowing, though just a bit.
Do you think language is anything like the sea?

The rain is wholly adequate and one can see
That the wind is precise. Words rain into the sea
And no words are drowning.
We gather here in groups. In the blowing
Wind words whistle pure and tender:
The sea forgets what everyone cannot remember.

Viggo Broendal: Danish speculative linguist of the early twentieth century.

Two Prose Poems

I

In what way is the stone a world? Not in the same way as dandelions are canaries which do not fly or waves are knives scraping across the beach. The stone is a world: note the wolf-like spider stalking lambs, the small tired flies which leave the edge of seaweed at closing time and listlessly drift homewards, in swarms. Can anyone endure that much? The stone in your hand is one thing, incredible and grotesque with large holes and its ridiculous appendix of dry seaweed; it leaves the hand and flies in its partial ellipse, like a comet, out and down towards the waiting splash, with its tail waving as wearily as the last wet handkerchief at the stern of an emigrant ship.

II

On sunny days the sea is divided into differently coloured areas, partly according to the nature of the bottom, partly according to the direction of the wind. But today the sea is grey, as grey as the sky and without any visible boundary between air and water, between the bluish milk and the porridge. No sharp boundaries: even the shoreline is ugly and rugged today. It annoys me. By keeping constantly on the move, constantly changing my vantage points and by alternately closing and opening my eyes, by using piers and jutting headlands and by covering the parts that don't fit with my hand, I try to produce increasingly pure configurations. Is that of no use? In fact I know it is in here *(indicates his breast)* where all the theorems are to be found, not only the solution of the equation but the equation itself. Once I may have believed that I would be able to find a form beneath this wet licentiousness, this criminal indifference to our laws.

Three Baroque Arias *from* Gradiva

I *Gradiva: Hanold Sings*

Such milky mildness shines forth only from the mouth of an archaic
    goddess
Such living limbs can, stonebound, shimmer only in the telescope of
    history reversed
Such eloquent temples can be taciturn only in terracotta coloured face
    against a freer firmament.
Freer than Medea of Pompeii in motherpain, in motherpride against
    sirocco-mutilated skies,
    triumphant,
Her sorcerer's wand pressed against an empty uterus,
Prouder than Prospero who gelded his own weapon of desire, denying
All his children the common act of freedom, the killing of the old king.

Seen against more sacred skies, in more limpid light, rather like Greek
    Helen,
Reflected not in language but in old men's bursting eyeballs

Göran Printz-Påhlson

In convex catatonia preserved through snowing centuries in the apocryphal
 time of conception,
Even in Teutonic Tannhäuser-woods, in the glimpse of shadow in the
 mirror of the study . . .

Such pride in her pace can only a goddess display, with perpendicular
 uplifted foot,
Arrested in her movement, immovable and travelling through the
 whirling fall of centuries.

II *Hanold's Last Dream*

She sat in the sun, with a snare
of grass, in the door of waiting.

Still, observe fluttering
            floundering things,
hold to the dream which tosses in your hand.

A bird fell to the deceitful
floor of the dream. The lizard fled.

Colleague, hunter, who then hunts?

III *Vertumnus: His Sestina*

When I am changed the young bud turns to leaf.
When I am changed the bare hills turn to vale
And when I breathe I turn to cotton cloud
The heavens which are mirrored in my eye,
And when I wander, I wander deep in woods
And when I close my eyes there is no sun.

At one time on the world there was no sun
And every soul was an unwritten leaf
In the middle of the dark Unchanging Woods.
On the Tiber's banks and in the Tuscan vale
I flew in every downy seed for I
Was born of wind and wind-begotten cloud.

A warrior who went prancing round the cloud,
A sower with his basket in the sun:
So was born this metamorphosis, this I;
Along the sunburned thighs there grew green leaves
And toes flowed down like water in a vale
To take quick root in some vast wondrous woods.

There went an apple-selling lady in the woods
Whose ancient features were as fuzzy as a cloud.
She reached the boundaries of fair Pomona's vale
And smiled at Beauty there as at the gallant sun.
She wished to kiss each green and dew-fresh leaf
Among the fruit. She loved and she was I.

A frightened girl—and also she was I—
Ran panting and pursued through darkening woods.
She stumbled and observed among the leaves
A black and curly head against the cloud—
Beneath the god surrendered to a violent sun
And then bark covered up her chaste womb's vale.

I remember once in a Thessalian vale
How straying lost in that strange province I
Perceived a glimpse as from a naked sun:
It was a crowd of women in the woods
Who in a panic clustered like a cloud—
Pale waiting chrysalis beneath the leaf.

On mountains, in the vale, at sea and in the woods,
There consumed am I as when a summer cloud
Annihilates a sun and closes all the leaves.

Gradiva: German novella by Wilhelm Jensen, analysed by Freud in a celebrated essay.

Vertumnus: Roman diety, referred to by Ovid (*Metamorphoses* xiv) and Propertius (IV : 2).

Göran Printz-Påhlson

Sir Charles Babbage Returns to Trinity College *After Having Commissioned the Swedish Mechanic Scheutz to Build a Difference Engine. On the Bank of the River Cam He Gazes at the Bridge of Sighs and Contemplates the Life of the Dragonfly*

No man can add an inch to his height, says the Bible. Yet once I saw the detective Vidocq change his height by circa an inch and a half. It has always been my experience that one ought to maintain the greatest accuracy even in the smallest things.

No one has taught me more than my machine. I know that a law of nature is a miracle. I know that a change of nature is a miracle. When I see the dragonfly, I see its nymph contained in its glittering flight. How much more probable is it that any one law will prove to be invalid than it will prove to be sound. It must happen in the end: that wheels and levers move accurately but that the *other* number will appear, the unexpected, the incalculable, when the nymph bursts into a dragonfly. I see a hand in life, the unchanging hand of The Great Effacer.

Therefore be scrupulous and guard your reason, in order that you may recognize the miracle when it occurs. I wrote to Tennyson that his information was incorrect when he sang 'Every minute dies a man,/Every minute one is born.' In fact every minute one and one-sixteenth of a man is born. I refuse to abandon this one-sixteenth of a man.

Man-Made Monster Surreptitiously Regarding Idyllic Scene *in Swiss Hermitage, a Copy of Goethe's 'Werther' Resting in its Lap*

It is sometimes considered to be an advantage to start from scratch. I myself would be the first to admit that my maker did a good job when he constructed my brain, although it must be said that he was unsuccessful with my outer appearance: my ongoing programme of self-education has provided me with many a happy hour of intellectual satisfaction. Spying on these touching family tableaux unobserved makes me nevertheless both excited and dejected. I suspect that only with the greatest of difficulties shall I myself be able to establish meaningful relationships with other beings. It is not so much my disfigured countenance which distresses me—

I have accustomed myself to *that* by gazing at it in a nearby tarn and now find it, if not immediately attractive, then, at least, captivating: in particular the big screws just under my ears which my maker insisted on putting there for God knows what purpose, accentuate my expression of virile gravity and ennui—as rather a certain lack of elegance and animal charm. It seems for instance to be almost impossible for me to find a suit that fits as it should. One of my more casual acquaintances, a certain Count Dracula, whom I vaguely remember having encountered in some circumstances or other—regrettably I cannot remember where or when—is in this respect much more fortunate: I envy him his relaxed manner of deporting himself in evening dress, but I have to admit that I cannot understand the reason for his negative (and extremely selfish) attitude to his environment. For myself, it seems as if my background and construction limit the possibilities for the successful development of my personality in socially acceptable forms. Evidently, I must choose between two possible careers: either to seek self-expression in the pursuit of crime—within which vast and varied field of activity sexual murder ought to offer unsurpassed opportunities for a creature of my disposition—or during my remaining years quietly to warm my hands at the not altogether fantastically blazing but nonetheless never entirely extinguished fires of scholarship.

Turing Machine

It's their humility we can never imitate,
obsequious servants of more durable material:
     unassuming
they live in complex relays and electric circuits.

Rapidity, docility is their advantage.
You may ask: *What is 2 × 2?* or *Are you a machine?*
     They answer or
refuse to answer, all according to the demand.

It's however true that other kinds of machines exist,
more abstract automata, stolidly intrepid and
     inaccessible,
eating their tape in mathematical formulae.

Göran Printz-Påhlson

They imitate within the language. In infinite
paragraph loops, further and further back in their retreat
    towards more subtle
algorithms, in pursuit of more recursive functions.

They appear consistent and yet auto-descriptive.
As when a man, pressing a hand-mirror straight to his nose,
    facing the mirror,
sees in due succession the same picture repeated

in a sad, shrinking, darkening corridor of glass.
That's a Gödel-theorem fully as good as any.
    Looking at in-
finity, but never getting to see his own face.

translated by the author

Turing machine: abstract automaton, first described by the British mathematician Alan Martin Turing.

Joe Hill in Prison

Memory: slapping sails in the harbour.
Skipper in calfskin gloves, his spyglass
pressed against a watery eye. Haze over Gävle's port.
Winter-grey days of refusal to thaw.
Then cannonades of ice-breaking and jubilation.
Spring with a song in its arms.

Work heavy as sodden clothes.
Tramping the Dust Bowl toward the Rockies.
Tramping with pocketfuls of borrowed years
over territory where only the water leaves tracks,
where the heat is a faded gold-brown in colour
and the birds speak with leathery tongues.

Looking through the bars (like a brother
from other centuries he never heard of
transported far off into the Finnish mountains). Writing a song.
Waiting and thinking, while the time idles along
like a night shift, over that which never even happened,
the futility in these methods

of taking, hating, and giving. Once life was
hard and clean as a handshake. Then
it became a mask with a stiffened grimace.
Waiting in the morning chill for the bolt to be
drawn from the door. Deadly fear blinking sleepily even now
in the bright light of martyrdom. It is done.

translated by Richard B. Vowles

Joe Hill: Swedish-American song-writer and labour organizer, executed at Salt Lake City in 1916.

GÖRAN SONNEVI

Abstract World

The street. Trees which
sprawl in pellucid air.
The people
walk past.
Their faces, white, cut through me.
Their bodies like lumps
in the light which pulverizes
stone.

Unfinished

I

The stone which shrinks and shrinks
becomes a fist of light, blinding
the senses.
        Blind life
closed in stone.

II

That the music!
        —bow of lightness
in a broken arch.
        —trees in metamorphosis!
The air transparent, calm.

Lake and Silence

It is sometimes said, very softly
that in autumn the swallows sink
to the bottom of the lake.
There all is still.

—Do they enter their sleep?
—Are they dreaming?

—In the dark water I saw
the light wings.

Landscape

The landscape has an invisible face.
How can I write joy?

Snow falls silently through the skin
downward in emptiness. How
can the face which does not know pain
show joy?

It is dark now, no snow is falling.
Ever more clearly
I feel the face. It has no features?—

February: Abstract Awakening

A morning, wakening
Trees beat against me through the window,
white fires.
        Death,
to expose this whiteness!

A bird came and went again.
Outside time.

        Trees, enormous,
forming the pain.

Göran Sonnevi

'Void which falls out of void...'

a

Void which falls out of void, transparent,
cones, hemispheres,
fall through empty space.
Thoughtform, crescent, trajectory.

b

However relevant!
In the infinite freedom I can
keep back, give
my notes resilience, in relation
to each other, to my whole body, which also
falls in infinity through empty space:
e.g.
Charlie Parker's solo in *Night in Tunisia* on May 15th 1953.

c

The flight of sentimentality through empty space.
Through its elliptical hole
an heraldic blackbird's
black wings, yellow beak, round eyes, with the yellow
ring, which defines its inner empty
space.

Hölderlin I

'Die Zeit ist buchstabengenau
und allbarmherzig'
said Hölderlin
in his last letter to his mother,
from Tübingen   In short

quick obsessively
interrupted letters
he tried
to retain the bond of life
with his mother, in everything else
submitted totally
to the world   An omen
of war is set
in the sky, a
sign of
light, which flashlike
delineates
the architecture of crystals, the
flowing
crystalline
architecture in violent change—
From this war
nobody is returning
except in silence, mute, literal, precisely
possible

Hölderlin II

Hölderlin didn't like peasants
When the serfs
revolted in Württemberg
he wrote home
to his mother
that she shouldn't worry
that one knew how
to take care of them
for sure
These revolts
were extensions of greater revolts
in the Jura in Switzerland
against the feudal order

Göran Sonnevi

which in their turn were extensions
of the French Revolution

Meanwhile Hölderlin dreamed
and worked to extend the revolution
also to Germany
He wrote
that he was ready to act
He was a kind of Jacobin

But the peasants, the allies
of the French Jacobins
and the base of their
military strength
were to Hölderlin
only coarse and repellent
His revolution
was enacted by
heroes of an idealized Hellas

His reality was hallucinated

*

Still so scintillatingly precise, vehement
like one's convalescence after
a period of fever, when the senses
cannot fend for themselves, when the brain
suddenly builds
wholly new categories
of perception, which enter
further into
new knowledge, new life

All his life Hölderlin was a fugitive
from everything else, from all
that did not constantly rest
in the point of ultimate love
until the tension no longer

could be maintained
The point which is present
beneath everything, everywhere
in the uttermost extremities
of space and time

*

The point which is inside
all life
before it is extinguished
It is also present
in everything else

Will You Please Come In and Put on a Hat!

What do I want with a hat?
It's just my head
that's cold!
Mother, come
and help me! My back's
cold too, mother,
and it's burning!
Pour water on it
and it comes out in flames!
Then you won't be cold.

Why should I come in?
The house is feeling cold.
Pour water on
it, so that it burns!
Mother, you're cold too.
You are quite
white and you don't burn. Here,
mother, you can
have my hat.
Then you won't be cold.

Göran Sonnevi

'Bloody cunt!...'

Bloody cunt!
can I take you home
tonight
The one who is outside the group
hasn't got a language
His imitations
become awkward, transparent
He is split
Strange antennae
grow out of him, his forehead
elbows, kneecaps
break out in the same
tissue as e.g. his ears and nose,
antennae with eyes at the ends, eyelashes
long, thin tentacles that
end in a silky thread,
others end in terror, bent by
pendulums,
whiskers, genitals—
It is his language
Who doesn't get his language
from Gideon Bibles, Hymnbooks, Walls
with Fuck and Cunt
For someone who knows nothing
of what's behind the language
language will be coarse
like the reality behind the language
The word *language* is not coarse
Fucking Nigger!
You are split
We split ourselves   you me I you
Asshole!
Motherfucker! Cocksucker!
Holes
We split
inexorably as one splits
somebody from below with an axe—

After Seven Lean Years

The war criminal McNamara
has now
left his post as
U.S. Secretary of Defense, and instead
emerged as
President of the World Bank—in the cold
spring light of 1968
During the autumn
elections were held for
the U.N. organization
for world food supplies, F.A.O.
After a long struggle
including political blackmail
against the candidate
of the poverty-stricken countries
a European from Holland
was elected
thanks to Swedish support
and with the blessing of the U.S.
The African candidate was unacceptable, for
through the World Bank
the U.S. controls the F.A.O. project
for the agricultural
development of Africa   And an unlimited
growth of food production in
hungry Africa
is also unacceptable, as it
would, according to U.S. predictions,
negatively change
the world market
So McNamara
has some work to do!
After seven lean years of genocide, with
no obvious success
he can calmly
look forward to seven fat years
without the crisis of conscience

Göran Sonnevi

which is forced
by the light of an open struggle

It Has to Work

It is difficult to repair
but it has to work
Otherwise we might as well die
all of us
But first the old
damaged parts must go
entirely, be dumped
into Hell where they belong
If one tries
to build on
crap, it will stay crap
Who selects
new parts? Who manufactures them?
We must do it
ourselves!
There are no blueprints
Then it may be best
to make everything new?
That much is clear
But there are only these people
who are here
worn, used up   And it has to work
And it won't work
without people
Even if most don't function that well
they are not crap
We are not crap

'A mother stands in front...'

A mother stands in front
of the buildings
of the unfinished nuclear power plant
She carries her child as protection
against the furious images
inside her body
The sea outside is grey
the earth grey
the child inside everything
is grey
The mother grey, waiting
for the slow
invisible pain

*

Some demand from us exact knowledge
of the unknown   A knowledge
they don't possess themselves
What we know with certainty
is that they do not know
That is exact knowledge

We know exactly that our future
can never become anything else
but a series
of approximations, a series
of probabilities
But that in the future our lives
will become wholly exact, wholly
dependent on
irreparable mistakes in
the computations, irreparable
mistakes in the biological
organization of our future lives
That is a kind of exact knowledge

*

Göran Sonnevi

We have a power in our hands to touch
all of mankind
at a distance
Distance also in time
in future time, touch
the unborn, bodies
not yet conceived
And we do not know
what we are doing
but shall not for all that
be forgiven   Not by anybody

*

We all stand like a mother
in front of the unknown child, the child
we knew
nothing about
We see it dying for everyone
It cannot die

The series of deficient children
will also stand like a mother
waiting
for yet another unknown child

Mozart Variations

        Mozart
lived with his death
present in the music, as
ultimate life, heightened
to the impossible, the
subtlety of impossible love
infinite subtlety, in movements
touch, faintest

indications of a smile,
in angles
of lines, in the limbs, with
the fingers
I touch your
back with
and you
reply   Then
I can
seek your mouth
and the body moves
in perfect
rhythm, dance

*

Incredible music!

so near
so near death
and life

life looks
at me
with clearer eyes

*

Music, you touch
my depths
and I cannot
explain you
(whatever purpose
would be served
by that)
Beginnings
of tears
which come
and I am cold

Göran Sonnevi

in spite of intermittent
sun, now
shadow

*

Alone, it
is so, only
I cannot
open myself entirely
without being
effaced, like the straight
white surface
where the processes
are projected
And yet
I want
it!

*

Come, human-tending
form, come
closer, see you
so far
away, I do not
know if you exist
except as
music, half
dreamed, clearly
carved in invisible
matter

And you, mankind, as
you are, with
infections
wounds, skin
which breaks open
even for

disease
Paralysing
death, with growing hair
in its mouth,
life, which
has grown wrong
and cannot
be put right

Irreparable you! Irreparable
music!
Incredible
you!

*

Music, you open up to hell
and paradise

music in dizzying
paths, which
lead straight
into the smile,
unexpected, alone, by
itself

and now, now, now
Where am
I on my way, this
time, for
which time in
my life?
Permanent
fear, permanent
diseases   And joy which
is never
permanent

*

Göran Sonnevi

darkness, hollowness, which closes
from outside, which is felt
also from inside   And how
can I see
the difference

Now you come
again,
so full of your own soft
fullness, a
ripeness, and fear
even to
the innermost taste
of the tongue

            Death
is not, exists
as ultimate
life, in the completion
of existence, when
the flash of light
comes, and everything
lets go

*

invade me, music, ultimate
life, death,
finely divided
in all of the body's
infinitesimal ramifications
at once!

GÖSTA FRIBERG

Nobody

Night between the trees
the lawns
the stillness of one single stroke of the clock—
The green bench under the street light,
there is nobody there: leaning against the back
with its air of night against the arm, and night
all the way to the ground. Nothing,
when one observes its essence,
seems to turn a mite
and change to Nobody . . .

There is only the absence there, sitting,
of somebody who has left long ago,

A mite leaning against the arm
surrounded by light.

The House of the Deaf and Dumb

Earth-wasp
you flew in shining through the long shadow of the eaves

past the house of the deaf and dumb in the woods
House of
Deaf
and Dumb, where all the lost ones were

And a Shadow, with a murmur of the soundless at its back
stood quite still, took one step
out of the door,
and gazed on after you

—with a strangely burning
silence round her head
she walked on after you

saw you travel toward worlds of light and voices

And you, resting on a twig, polishing your wings,
vibrate back
dark air . . . cover her with such dark air
down there, where she walks under the trees,

beautiful, incessantly beautiful
in the invisible.

The Road

> . . . *that the thread of sparks will remain unbroken*
> —Robert Bly

Road I travelled on.
And it
would soundlessly take me down into its ground,
take me on its way.

                There
would only exist
air
which moved between the trees, air
which travelled between the trees—

with the faint
barely visible
beginning
of the features of somebody else . . .

Gösta Friberg

                In the same place,
with the same movement forward,
now walking. With a whistle
clear in the night
to some bird. Or just alone, walking.

Nobody else around . . .
where that man is walking.

The spark between worlds, lives—
        and the silhouette of a back
disappearing through the woods.

*

the light recumbent, resting on a cloud

with   underneath

only

        groundblindness

straight down

the silence
where we are annulled
—as simple
weightless
necessary
as
nothing

The Growing

> *The world actually lives because it combines earth and heaven, night and day, death and life.*
> —Erich Neumann

> *Is man the most valuable of all things?*
> —Gary Snyder

Two, three generations in our time
are busy changing the foundations of all light,
plant after plant is extinguished
making for a black, sterile planet ...
the small split concentrations of atomic sunpower
trickle out in forest brooks, killing the forest.
Which makes the splendid quantities
of work by hand and body
with the earth
so meaningless. Which makes us meaningless.
Devonian, Jurassic, Cretaceous, Eocene
are breaking down: the tissue of their lungs
no longer can supply the sea with oxygen. Radiata
dancing through the mud of the Indian Ocean
radiate no longer
light from their small graceful skeletons of silica ...
The face of the Tertiary age gradually changes out of forests
to a cancerous black mass: its temples broken up
by radium: blue algae
which infuse the earth with oxygen, in rainbreathing
commerce with Brazilian forests, are suffocated
underneath the thin oil films of the seas.
And the bees whose balance is disturbed, who mistake the flowers
in the meadow, stand still in sunlight
          with trembling, decomposing wings ...
fly straight into the mountains
and try to eat directly from the walls the pollen of black rock—
deranged in their behaviour
like patients

Gösta Friberg

in a ward for ECT.
All because we have blocked up
the natural breathing of the cycles
with protection of our stony western cities: slammed
shut great bank-vault doors into the future
and the past: Because we'll kill it all, everything—
while we, schizophrenic guardians
at the dragonhoard of our technology, more and more
become deranged in our behaviour: armed with H-bombs
and machine guns helter-skelter: Star
of Pentagon in solar systems
waste it, before it wastes the earth.

Lead us away . . .

*

The long work of the past with the earth:
Seed vessels, blowing across the plains, unconscious
of the seas of light
they open in the unborn lives . . . Grass tongues
bent backwards by the sun. Beavers mating by the river.
The stoat, licking fish scales from its paws,
which flows away among the rocks . . . An antique golden coin,
    Hadrian's frozen profile,
touched by the past.
Bodies fleeing to escape the suffocation
in volcanic ashes raining on Pompeii. Green lungs of Amazonas:
oxygen which breathes us when we walk
the roads in Hälsingland.
    The blue-grey back of the hare—
a disappearing colour cutting through the summer woods . . .
Gift of calm, unruffled silences: because the inner being
of us all is one. The distant
fire,
resting in the sun and stars,
which, far beyond geology, reached the earth
and made the dark brown feathers of the horned owl,
    yellow streaks across the chest,
that's perched in the shade of the rock face.

Cold water, taste of iron.
Resinous fine wood, tinder, little elfin gift
that's found to warm the fingers.
The slow sun of forest brooks. Bread. Rain,
organic with the earth.
          Everything was work.

     Crystal jellyfish
rising and sinking, swimming their bells
in the quiet of the nightly ocean . . . Beginning
of eclipse
as shadow first appears at the edge of the sun disk . . .
The web.
Black eiderdown on shining points of silver
of the granite rocks. Islets far away, nearly invisible,
soundlessly gravitating their spring . . .
      The light's
strength in Sherpa Tensing's movements across Himalayan slopes
when he carried the unconscious Hillary to the top.
Silence, cold.
The mating calls of whales, deflected by the rounding of the earth beneath
    the sea.
And plankton floats, borne by currents of the sea,
which through millennia made visible
Orion on our retinas. A Shaman
                      bending to the sandpaint
refractions of the crystals
in his hands:
'Lean your ear to the pollen, hear how they sing . . .'
And the strange thing that the earth, from underneath,
can support—
The raised, striding legs of moose which disappear in mist . . .
Steaming excrement,
forest paths, the eggs of the glow-worm shining
on a leaf in the dark . . . Everything was work.
Everything was work,
to make something grow.

  *

Gösta Friberg

Protect the great and magic parts of the earth: forests,
animals, oceans, plants. We must protect them
in this decade, give them all the power that we can.
Protect the strong and weak lights of the firmament,
so that they can unexpectedly
be found
in the eyes of the unborn. Protect the daylight whose invisible energies
    vanish in waves
across the tops of fir trees . . .
If there was nothing there
to meet the rays from below,
they would continue
straight on downwards
in enormous blackness . . .

*

The entirely beautiful
tiny face of the ant
next to a spruce needle—
and she takes hold of the needle, coaxing
its green splendour to its place

                      on its back,
carries it home.

*

    the earth's
    faintly glowing
    egg
    on a leaf.   And the glow-worm
curved around it—like the weak, faraway
  light from our Galaxy: The Giving-of-Birth.

      The Growing.

TOBIAS BERGGREN

Poem from Gotland, 1 Sept. '73
in Memoriam Salvador Allende

A day with boredom and unsuccessful verses and to begin again
Now evening, seven degrees centigrade, dark, northerly winds
An approach light winks to me without confidence
It will rain tonight
My child is falling asleep, asks
Why it is possible to fly in dreams
A chilly day has come to an end
Tonight Allende will be murdered
Still I know nothing
I cannot even fly towards the west
Thoughts of starving continents like deepfreeze counters in the brain
Blood and vapour
The red pattern dissolves
Out there the north wind moves like an animal among nettles

Out there people are looking for some place to sleep
Something to eat
Some kind of meaning
I am not happy but I shall survive the night
Communism isn't happy tonight but that unhappiness will pass
Things like murder will pass in this case
Something that the killers never do understand
But why don't they just go ahead quickly and shoot themselves

No one is hurt by my hatred on the other side of the earth
The approach light winks knowingly
As if I was about to lose control of myself as well
Dividedness
Dividedness and coldness
Not to lose control of ourselves
We must work for the abolition of political control
Not daring to leave all political power to the people
We do not trust ourselves
Which is insane: we have no other power than our own to trust

They who are without trust shatter socialism
Tonight the killers will enter the cracks once again

The beam from the approach light divides and divides
Dreams of flying are being dreamed
Tonight we are alone like animals in the dreams of a chrysalis

Socialism hurts in the back of the world
Where Chile's narrow wing is growing

In the Mountain: Part II

(Voice of the traveller)

The voices around me slowly fall silent
and the atmosphere changes . . .
I walk the streets, it is like an ordinary
September Sunday in an ordinary
city . . . Rapidly drifting clouds, wet and clear . . .
I have the feeling, suddenly, that
from this world an atmosphere is easily dispersed . . .

And meetings that one shares with a stranger in the street
may suddenly lead one, through murmurs and suggestions, into
the light of another time . . .
And suddenly I am on the other side of myself:
I have travelled in a gesture that somebody casually
made to me in the middle of the street . . .

I am standing on some huge marble steps and I know
that they are the steps
which lead mankind
from deep under ground to galleries
where the sky is hanging from the wall
wet mirrors for a life of blood and clay or
magnificent paintings
depicting the desirable life that is led by demonstration objects . . .

Tobias Berggren

Before me, in front of the steps, the plaza is empty, windy,
sand is blowing dryly in the light
A stage: and now the actors enter! Two executioners
and a man completely naked
Quickly, without any fuss, they lead him to the middle of the plaza
and begin immediately to flay him
alive. Dirty seagulls assemble
their cries mingle with those of the man being flayed. The light
flickers mechanically like a clock. An ancient arithmetic
here has vanquished
nature . . . And the surfaces of things
slowly begin to burst,
like singed tin foil, and their immateriality seethes out of them.
like darkness
derived from speeds faster than light! I breathe
into my body immateriality. A darkness
comprises all light . . .

Beyond this uncanny place
large ships glide across nocturnal waters
and disappear
shining of light and laughter,
glide on past this summary place where life is archivized
in the light of a discontinuous glare . . .
Unknown transports knock against each other in the dark
Unknown: like animals of night in the shadows of the earth . . .
Hearts of the moon, almost life, dreams of other beings . . .
of human beings in human dreams . . .

The flayed man
calls out to the ships on the water
They reply sadly like tethered stars

*

. . . And people deeper in the shadow of the street
are dressed in doghead patterned clothes—
signs of prohibition against being in the sun
They walk on rapidly, rocking

and nervously four-fingered hands
grope out after mine when I approach
the edge of shadows
'Shhhhh,' they say, 'let us touch your face!
Your sign is so warm!
You understand that what is mask out there for us is ikon'

A gesture in the street
makes me oddly empty
and suddenly prepared
to humour or indulge these creatures
The skin stiffens on my face
It is cold, extremely cold, and suddenly I realize:
The difference between light and shadow
is enormous in this world
Cold as carbonic acid snow is the air of shadow-dwellers
And their sounds: entirely different: doghead
patterned people's voices ring
like smelted tin in freezing water, notes
from crystallizing processes unseen, hard & bursting
What world is this? Does it belong to those
fallen from all memory?
To those withdrawing from the present? Suddenly
the snow begins to fall
A coldness crystallizes blood and freedom
A freezing hollowness invades
all words as if the words were coarsened beaks
where whispers seep like dangerous gas
from those eternally forgotten
'And still you live! and warm you dwell
in others' memories
That is why your face, although contorted
out of pretence there
by us is worshipped as a sign
of freedom that's self-evident'
And the chorus of voices reaches me on my terrible
border between crystallization
and slavery,
my life...

Tobias Berggren

'O sacred, O five-fingered warmths,
Intrepid, shed for us the mask
O man your sign
Your truth
Is ours! Slavery withdrawn
In petrifaction
And only thus
In crystallization
And death . . . !'

And I am drawn to them
Into their world that flutters leafy shadows
round me: hands, cold hands, touch
me tentatively, and with intentionalities in the
intentionless expression fluttering
clothes, ragged & ethereal, half dissolved
stream past
Deceiving, redolent
cool creatures come up close to me, tentative
touches of paws, noses, muzzles
sudden laughter
which is *forced over my head*, I laugh, milk-
white air trickles from my mouth, a
face turns upward and meets my laughing breath
It groans: creatures
which seem made of thin diaphanous fabric
spin their light mouths towards me
From soft and downy orifices tongues come out
which feel their way
under my collar, down across my chest, belly,
lick my sex, and penetrate me from behind,
cackling, chattering . . .

Something else is inside me
It whispers: 'You are another, another, another . . .'
I watch myself in a mirror which is handed over:
I look like some obscene sign
And the mirror dissolves giggling above me
It becomes a tunnel of light

I travel in it, I am a seed,
A sperm
among billions of others, blind, open
for billions of possibilities . . .

Larvae of loneliness and dread:
But the only possibility for this world:
Eggs open their living mouths
and give birth to the planet . . .

*

(Song from outside)

'What does the heavy earth know . . .
which is laid in the night like an egg
hatched by your eyes every morning . . .
Will their warmth last, warmth of eyes,
throughout the night . . . '

Poem about Time, by the Sea

I

Underneath my shadow on the limestone rock
a two-thousand-year-old seal hunter is slowly
disappearing toward the routes of the stars
I am his shadow
in the light of the blue-weed

And the light of the sea, of the water
which dazzlingly filters all connections, dissolves
earth's hard dependencies in pelagian fantasies
vegetating frequencies, the extended
dreaming *Vagantenlieder* of the schools of herring
for the bones of the drowned
which spell the sign of Continuity

Tobias Berggren

The light of the sea
which projects my shadow towards the stars

What wave brought me here? That of the drowned?
The wave of the already drowned—reflecting the sign of Pisces—
at least was visible, *that* wave
was for one and only one: 'she is for me' and
he draws a deep breath: 'it was never her' and sinks
with the boat, is eaten
and annihilated: the atom furnaces
of Pisces
are opened in his brain,
eels, codspawn now
go touring in his ragged bony eyes—
You, in the sign of the Fisherman,
reflect
with algae in your heart, the wind in your summers,
here is one
who once was also five years old
and picked the pine-cones in the pine woods
who was only five and lowest in the pecking order
Now is eaten
a tenderly considered
human being
by currents and molluscs
Now Man is eaten

Now where she rests under the surface of photographs
by her face of stone
which inexorably portrays
a fearful, a mortally fearful
species, unknown
heavily and dangerously unfamiliar . . .
The heavenly hens are guarding

II

The clock is ticking, the waves of the sea
and the rustling leaves of the trees

move in this life, where cries and songs
rock through my skull
Time is up, is the work done? never
did I think so little
could be accomplished in so long a time, the leaves
do more and devastate nothing
The clock is singing its absolute song
to the trees rocking in wind from the works of man
Time is not like the clock
Time is uneven, and full of energy
it is dispersed around
people, we grope for it with clicks and wheels
as we grope for light & day with doors & windows & fingers, but
we waste the world
in the alchemy of retention

In the alchemy of returning we devastate the world

For everything is movement and movement is change
and not the swallows, the electrons or the nimble grasses
not the disintegrating nations nor
the Medusa-like damp stain on the wall of the summer cottage
not the exploding stars nor you
are reality
outside the net of connections rocking
back and forth for cries and songs, time out there
exists in a dog's heart or in roots of the submarine mountains
or anywhere, and in myriads—but the stars
turn on their axes of human matter, and the seas
can do nothing without their coastal dwellers, and fishermen
nothing with their nets but make symbols, and the nets
of connections nothing
with the ticking scales of the clock
which are scattered
in the grass where the children play

The grass can split the atom furnace
but man can never begin again

Tobias Berggren

III

The inventory of the coast . . .
Among the chattels also human bodies
This broken home—
You approached me on the beach, happy I was . . .
you left me: a beach
from which one is relentlessly taken, from which
my body disappears with the tide
O I have been waiting turned towards the sea
my face in the light, in the light of the horizon, and
my back in hell
Can you see my back in the dark?
Here it is, here in what is written,
here
In the place where I write down my memories of you

I looked on the limestone rock and found
the rusty iron nail
on which you cut yourself
Your blood was still there
A yellow lichen had grown from it

LARS NORÉN

Solitary Poem

A final
time
strikes
through the sky

—When it
opens:
take a seat, and
listen, empty it
with your mouth, as they
emptied the latrines

A Dresden
stands
on the hill
and detains
the face
of the grass,
of mathematics

You and
you, solitary,
where do you
come home? who
keeps together the
bestial house which
we cannot keep?

A language
consumes us,
a rain
eats us.

Syringe

I came together with
all of you looking for my purity,
and my purity
I looked for in everything,
but especially in soap,
and then, when it was not to be found there,
in things falling apart or inviting me,
in the broken radio
in her ass
which opens up like a
soft pistolshot of muscles
But for some time
I am cut off from all things and
friends by a spontaneous void
The digits which instead
I collect suddenly give off
an *indescribable* warmth.

31 Words about Flanders

In Flanders
The horsemen are sitting
Like stuffed categorical imperatives
In gasmasks, helmets & with spears
The horses chew
From their feedbags, wink
Slowly at flies.
Afterwards delight
Speaks in tongues.

Lars Norén

From Dresden

In their zinc bathtubs they die
Like people burning.
The firestorm
Like a mother carries the children
In its right arm. The bird
Stands in the conflagration of air.
Above itself
It is dying.

I Burn My Lamp in the Meadow

I burn my lamp in the meadow.
I'm sitting in the white
darkness, in the flutter of diurnal harvest,
drinking my stillness with earthen hands.

Heartbeats reach far away into the home,
dead and blown away.

Today, the Rage for Harmony

Today, the rage for harmony. I
Play with animals in my head.

Still, there are short,
Steep, chthonic
Days, when the stone's
Heat comes from its inside:

Peace, imperative
Intensity, vulnerable
And fertile like
The fontanelle of morning.

Evening

Fruit is falling in space
(And the space is a room).
The fruit, vaster than space,
Envelops the room.

Below me: an irregular
Town around the annihilation: a
War-angel's innermost coat.

The Sphere of the Roads

I walk around the room,
Until the face extinguishes itself.
I speak the night until it grows.
The wings end in the mouth, go silent.
Here my heartbeats are counted down
To the singlehanded justice of the womb.

Allusions

Tonight the music
Is God's breath. He who knows
Mows the streets.

It falls flexible
Like the earth of mental clinics,
Flutters strong & stronger
Over my hands.

Lars Norén

Endpoem

Peaceful day which
Devours

Peaceful speech
In which to be annihilated
When it's resurrected

Peaceful night which
Tends the day's solitude
& the forehead's dust

Conclusion

I open and
Close my head
As I wish.

Now it
Doesn't fall.

It whispers
At last
The leaves of morning,
Wet & grey.

I see the day—
Animal in my palm.

It stands there
Eating the dream

August

1

The stones are hot.
The cattle are lowing.
The long-clothed infants flutter down
With a drop of milk in their mouths.
The smoke billows,
Dense pleated smoke
Or the thin flesh
Which rises still,
Smoke from unused honey
Or smoke from fires in trees,
It rises,
It brings down the subterraneans.

2

Girls and dogs
Sleep in the grass
Life is
A heartbeat
From my own
      The burning cattle
With tonsured skulls
Have come home
To their quivering stable.

3

Today I see that my daughter
Is higher, greater
Than I, and completed ... Her
Hard Kaiser head encircles me and carries
Me and helps me. We speak
Silently in each other and then
She paves the dead ones.
      She comes towards me in her Kaiser skirt.

Lars Norén

From the crib of the road
In a dust cloud of sleeping crickets,
Her large blue eyes are watching
How the realm of day binds its book.
      She hungers after herself.

from Wednesday October 17th

... the Swiss clocks depart
like birds in February
and a young mother walks the staircase
to the nursery with bread and milk
and the children small and clattering sleep
with a drop of ether in their eyes
The winter fisherman is dragged down
into the water and shouts out
Works and letters drift away
It is the two hundredth birthday,
it is the love story of autumn, do not read
the last chapter, save it
until it is best
In the village of Los precisely where
the 4,000,000-volt cable crosses
the road to Ljusdal near the church
the engineer has perched
with his bare hands touching the wires
Across bridges and other crystal places
nature is lovely today and has uncannily few
points of reference. Roads, railway tracks,
telegraph lines, electric wires
Everything is so beautiful, wide open
in the midst of the quotidian
                Do you believe in it?

*

I seek you, to cover
my thoughts with . . . and simple houses
Three nurses in the wind   anaesthetic
beauty and intelligence
But now screens have been put up around the sleeper
The sensuality of the housekeeper has laid
a dinner table on the burning ground
Afterwards I start dying more logically
Often I think of John Berryman
Why of him? Not because he died
—Jumping from bridges, is that
a brighter end to one's life
And the apples are now too ripe, start smelling of shit
Let's ring granny and ask how to preserve them
—I remember a book that I
haven't read, written by a French psychologist,
it was called *Dreams under Hitler* I think
and described how even in the case of the most ordinary people
the thoughts of Hitler & Fascism penetrated into their beings,
        into their dreams, into everything
one did, into everything one thought and acted
Today we live with dreams under Nixon
in blank hard aggressive rooms
with the left foot of the child Jesus
—This is as you notice no reason
able poem
I write because I have taken
a long walk with my child
from Stadshuset to Västerbron and then back
and have not seen anything at all. Better or worse
to be together inside the flesh in
the abyss of light. What is pure death
which passes by, who am I
in absolute darkness, why do I say the dead
when I don't think of the murdered
the ice cold slot, the murdered who
go on digging their latrines & then make everything of time
and let it through. Luna 18 crashes down
in the Sea of Fertility and Nina Khrushchev caresses

Lars Norén

her husband for the last time on the forehead
as in another diary some years ago
I am always welcome in this house
I can sit in a chair thinking of rivers
of doors, of physics, of the neighbours
who live above us, of somebody calling
his dog before going out into the darkness
falling, or of Peter Tillberg's
wonderful painting of the blue summer sky
in Titti's room, or a hot day
the caterpillars eating the leaves of the forest
and that, like yesterday, there are girls
one wants to clout because they think they're so beautiful
        and are so beautiful
in spite of the fact that one does not desire them, that
perhaps I should sleep with my wife
and that it is nice like going down
in cold water up to the genitals
        Sometimes I live in the strange room
like a sleeping bee in the cell of its honeycomb
or like a foot, like Vaslav Nijinsky's
fat and ageing foot which he bared
when at last the visitors left
in short: like something which is over
and people pass, careless and
helpless. In the dusk is revealed
slowly the indescribable earthen room
where the stone chairs are invisible
but where I want to approach more closely than here
        my hidden experience
Nowadays I hardly ever enter
that room, I sit here
with an experience of time common
to nearly all
The little wasp enters the bright skin of the zeppelin
The flock of swallows crawls across the glass
        of the Lancaster bomber
The cattle are stunned but not yet stung
grazing in the meadow

The puritans guard the wooden doors of the chapel
with pitchfork and scythe and
a bowl of milk with the same mournful skin
which clouds their solemn eyes
        I am and I am and I am
and bleed
from serious wounds
not belonging to me, they belong
like my eyes to somebody else
who laughingly listens to an annihilation incapable
        of going anywhere else

JAN ÖSTERGREN

Words

1

When I write words
I don't mean silent
snowflakes on slate-
warm roofs,

I mean
indoors: Firewood. Everybody's
his own tiled stove   we
smoke for a while
before we can warm up
the others

    before we
can follow the smoke
through your soft
filter, cloud of words

2

To live is
to take risks
somewhere an-
chored at the bottom
of language

the retreat back-
wards towards all
circumstances'
rock bottom
beginning

pry open
the blue mussel

when she rock-
silent keeps
shut

break
your gob
halfway out of joint
in the oyster-
bank

3

Deeply inside
I believe
in the words

the nuances
the prac-
ticalities

Yes:
we notice
broom by its smell
—in spite of all
this prattle
about yellowness!

listen to our
songs: smell of flowers
groping out of
the larynx

lips
in darkness: read them

Jan Östergren

Love

    When
I write love
I don't mean
Goethe's 150-year-old
sleight of hand: the quill
as bootjack

and not the Spanish
cloak under which
passion rises with the
rank of ensign

I mean:
the little fugue
squeezed through the
teeth of the organ—soon to be free!

sonata
for winds
and clouds

2

Keeez me hot meezter
she said blue with cold, lips
like candied violets

Zing de lazt danzz
she said later on
and started to
take off her clothes

Baby Doll
eager on the
outside but

deep inside chaste
as a display window   wanted

only her innocence back

become new
like a season : every
winter new ice
on the canal

3

Our desire
a dipping butterfly
which we catch, own
for a moment

        our

brain
a free habitation
for the softest
whims

        we

can afford
that
luxury

        our

heart
in one
single pulse-beat
we strike through
fall asleep under

open skies
tonight

4

Childwoman
with desires

Jan Östergren

swimming in your
inner oceans

let us probe
the deep
with each other

You have depth
I have plummet
and weights

we who have shared
the slumber of the child
heavy and warm
in the diving bell

let us return
to the surface: con-
quer the world
together

you have winds
I have sails

5

Let us disembark
across the drawbridge bent
like a backbone under
the past

let us forget
the past

let us build
each other new
at the shoreline

: a
gothic arch

which weightless
catches rhythms
of the flute

Death

1

Once you wanted
to talk about life
& started with death

: *Blue Gillette,*
the powerless words
in the bathroom cupboard

Paul Celan !

you taught me
to weigh life
on scales of gold : it had
to be right !

even if we lie
a gram here & there
we have to preserve
It All

: death,
a torpedo
in the net of the trawler

a weightless
autonomous   a
sexless sex

a lifebuoy?

Jan Östergren

2

*Your laughter is a dagger
honed for Garcia Lorca*

In a stable
with whitewashed stalls
I heard a
donkey bray

as mangily
       as brutishly
as laughter
in a crematorium

will never forget
my delight
when I thought: this
ought to be brayed out
every Sunday for
centuries
to come

would have saved us
many an evangelical
flight

PETER ORTMAN

Naughtnaught

Naughtnaught what is it the sphere
You carry on your shoulder

The rosy-cheeked apple
Where the worm is calling

Naughtnaught what is it the ball
You carry on your shoulder

The acne-infected moon
Where the moon dog is howling

Naughtnaught what is it the globe
You carry on your shoulder

The destruction-doomed earth
Where Naughtnaught is whispering

Naughtnaught what is it the atlas
You carry in your breast

Naughtnaught what is it
The sphere

Certain Days

Certain days Naughtnaught is terribly wise
He doesn't know any longer what to think

The lord of the fruit fly on the stone
The uniformed eye

The conceptual system
Word-nipples   tonsures

Lungs of colour-sergeants
Rain in the bamboo piano

Tulips in the park
With rosy complexions

Certain days Naughtnaught is terribly stupid
He doesn't know any shorter than he

Dreaming from
Blue-purple cotton clouds

A small small man in a corn-yellow hat
Who shouts thunder from the stage

The mountains are harvested
O friends in the eye of god

Praise and adoration to
The Heavens from the deep

Prose Poem

An old man comes walking very slowly into the supermarket and buys a packet of King-size Camels.

'Last night I dreamed that I was a runaway snake charmer,' he says to the cashier.

She says nothing.

'Don't be afraid,' he says. 'It's just empty talk.'

He puts his change in his coin purse. 'Tonight I am going to dream about you.'

Through the window she sees him open the packet and light a cigarette. Their eyes meet. He walks slowly away between two groups of high-rise flats.

Peter Ortman

Prose Poem

Get myself darker glasses. That's what I'll do. I don't want to melt any more eyes. Tired of these eternal deaths by drowning.

When I went home on the underground, a very beautiful blind man sat down in front of me. He felt something that obliged him to produce a small pamphlet in braille and furiously feel his way through it. I turned away and read my paper

tired of all these pointless encounters. Not to speak of this exaggerated romantic self-esteem which has come over me as a compensation for all the lost relationships worthy of *'realism'*

Realism

R e a l i s m
What is that

It is a difficult concept
It 'slides from your grip like a slippery eel'
It is Everything and Nothing

Everything and Nothing
Like a slippery eel

>   They came from a party in South Bend
>   Two cousins on a motor bike
>   When a moose ran across the road
>   That was a bloody ending

Everything and Nothing
Like a bloody Eel

Nothing Particular

Nothing particular to say tonight
dismal, dismal—orange juice has gone off

and the misery grows without my help
perialism, apitalism, lienation, ascism, etishism

ruin is near (as always) and the fridge is full of
presumably poisonous . . . hard times, hard times

but still as exceedingly careless one
furiously parts one's hair

pays one's homage to Nothing
falls with a heavenly gesture, KERPLUNK

while a man in green gumboots drags
his locked bicycle over the ice; thinking

arms, cunts, muffs, and pumps are so
obsolete these days

like a seam on the rump like Saul on David like
me dreaming of snails carrying their houses over the road

suddenly intensely crowded by these possessed
nuns on more yellow tandems, pursued

by a similarly obsolete animal with
a burning light blue tongue

but, think if it is or will be
as one believes

in the suburb there is a German in yellow shoes
thinking of *Mutti, Mutti*

so dismally blue
so dismally yellow

Peter Ortman

so goddamn fucking lonely tonight
old love-forsaken boozebody

the clock is ticking with the poem read on the radio
the bunch of grapes is drying on the plate

the poet speaks of arms like branches; but
somewhere he is always outside

young and spotless—it was long ago
I was made so nervous by poetry

THIS IS OUR ONE AND ONLY NIGHT
LET THE BUTTOCKS HEAVE

there is no end
to poetry

now I'm going off to the Café Christina
where there are as always some incredibly pretty girls

fresh as budding flowers
roses etc.

there are ten, there are perhaps eleven
o the speechless shivering

which is for all
of them

what am I thinking of
old ticking body, twitching

nerve
spotless soul

there is no end to poetry
there is no door to my heart

dismal
dismal

o youth like me
like me, like me

but listen
but listen

my tapdancing shoes
are still tapping

today
today today today

old and spotty, with arms like branches
now I turn off

JACQUES WERUP

Poet Tranströmer and the Rest of Us

My eyes are already the eyes of my grandchildren.
Perpetually I dwell in the yellow photographs of time.

Before Poet Tranströmer thrusts his quill into language sitting at his heavy
    mahogany desk
he has to get dressed in his brilliant green silk robe
with his lacy shirt with its eye-shaped tie pin
and crown himself with an imitation periwig *à la Goethe*.

The quotidian can never harm my eyes.
The one thing I distrust is noise: a deeper sleep.

Napoleon and Hitler are shaking hands on a dusty daguerreotype
and behind them you see Charles Dickens, photographer Tranströmer's
    stage designer
painting the scenery, a rolling summer landscape. But the photographer
    is cross:
the meadow is supposed to be Lepanto and Vietnam at the same time.

Stillness and simplicity both are like death.
Yes, we make noise. To be able to sleep, to forget.

Meteorologist Tranströmer and his assistant Verlaine notice the rain.
Rain, rain, and more rain.
All the world's diaries are being destroyed by rain.
Their texts all turn to pabulum.

The world is a mirror image of our forgetfulness.
In the office blocks one has decided on hieroglyphics.

Eleven-year-old Tranströmer, playing marbles, hears from his benign uncle
    on the radio
that there are still people willing to speak of the future,
and pay homage to some other uncle who may be occupied negotiating
    peace.
But this is a lie as blatant as an open door.

We do not dare to live without turning familiar quotations into our own
    offprints,
without changing twenty-pound notes pretending documentary credit.

Cars ARE perambulators! The friends of daddy (the grownups) lie about
    everything!
Motorist Tranströmer, playing with cars, learning to walk, is furious.
Why do people have to be so bloody self-important
just because they're a few inches taller?!

Only with the help of a more precise terminology for sorrow
can we comfort each other in this world.

There are no wars! No peace! We need no other language
but to throw butterflies at each other in order to know
how equally impossible collectors of ornaments we all are, shrieks Poet
    Tranströmer
pulling his quill out of the language which collapses like a premature
    apricot soufflé.

Who got the idea that life and death are two different things?
It's all going yellow now. NOW. ALL THE TIME.

'I could just as well go somewhere else'

I could just as well go somewhere else,
    there's nothing here which resists it,
    the seconds slide as easily into me
        as I slide out of them.
  Hopeless industrial compounds and council houses,
      ice-cold snow and rain,
    screeching and bumping of trains and
        booming loudspeakers
on windy platforms of the rural stations.
            And so?
    I don't have to stop,

Jacques Werup

        I play a different social part
     from most of those
            who sit and feel important
with wire netting round their lives,
        Jacques Werup, trembling hands,
superfluous and indifferent, with soft rain
          the only weather of his heart,
on eternal journey between his private neuroses,
     one of the intellectuals
    the western world can dispense with,
         superannuate and present with a gold watch.
Pressing his nose against the rain-drenched
                compartment window
     and Paul Verlaine appears on it
  like a misty reminder,
        that over the largest parts of the earth
    people curse their lives,
    all ideas seem at once
equally important or irrelevant.
        My love,
  give me more resistance, I would take part, why
    doesn't it hurt any more
always to travel away?
          On the sorrowful road
   away from each other
       it has always felt most obvious, near,
do you die when nothing hurts any more?

from Spots, Life

II   *Spots, Menace*

Dusk descends on half-finished
road works, abandoned petrol stations,
soldiers try in vain to start
a very run-down engine.

The birds sing in space
and in other solar systems, 'Mine
this is mine, mine, mine.'
People squat, glued to
their blood, to their fenced-off bits
of ceramic and silver. Children gnaw
the bark from blackened trees,
rain and magpies hinder vision,
where do the howling objects wish to be?

Your warm skin, your soft sex
in this room are joy, in this room
is freedom and peace and no one
disturbs us with weeping.
My love, not everybody suffers now
on this earth, on the earth people die
while we make love here in the room.
The economy weaves us in its net
in this room, on this earth.
Can our love be sequestered
in the room, on the earth?

You ask me where I am,
I do not know.
What I am, who I am
I do not know
if you ask me in that way.
But if you ask me
whose I am,
then I know, then I know
where I am, what I am
and who I am
if you ask me in that way.

You know that the Reptiles
return Hundreds of times

Jacques Werup

Hundreds of times.
Now they come
but they do not see you,
you protect yourself
by surrendering yourself.
You are No One,
nothing belongs to you,
you have no memories,
no friends, no language,
no eyes, no hands,
no future.
You protect yourself
by being owned,
by being Un-Natural,
infertile sand.

———

Humanity is not far away.
Interrupted letters in typewriters.
Half-eaten helpings on tables in cafés.
Flysheets not yet dissolved by the rain.
Escalators whirring between empty,
brightly lit floors of department stores.
Caftans left lying
on the cold stone floors of cathedrals.
Banknotes hurriedly gathered
beside the cash registers.
Toy trains humming in nurseries.
Red lamps still flashing
outside the abandoned boardrooms.
Implacability is not far away.

———

The conquered provinces:
swamps, karstlands,
scorched and windy.
The still unvanquished ones:
suburbs where nothing is produced
save for sleep and suicides.

The signals are approaching,
the crankshafts turn.
Those who watch and wait in rooms
close their eyes
in front of walls and windows.
Outside windows: the suburb;
an histological diagram
of an immense tumour.
Behind walls: the neighbour;
a rejected image
of your own despair.

XIV Spots, Silence

Against my window-pane, rain and leaves
A spider, long since dead.
The sound of weeping and retreat.
The odour of wet overcoats.
Some rusty spanners.
I observe these pale signs
from inside my crowded room,
they touch me as a lightness,
minus signs from inside me, mine.
Signs which deprive me of my life,
which balance my body and mind.
Signs which hasten my impulse to
Silence, the only thing that lasts.

Real freedom,
the one not limited
by an official Freedom,
infidel, mute, ambiguous,
like a crumpled piece of paper
it flutters around
among the granite languages,
fickle and without direction,
like a pinioned swallow
it spirals down

Jacques Werup

among the heavy statues,
memorials of confidence,
like a spent message
out of the last Throat.

───────────

Not even my love can
warm my sealed room,
not even my dream
demands more than silence.
How shall I put up with
the multitude of clamouring
crowds and armaments?

───────────

Both the static of your cells
and the creaking axles of the universe
are inscribed in the braille of the trilobite,
the indomitable structure
on which social orders rest.
We make journeys in imagination,
and we make real ones, to nowhere,
nowhere we escape
this veined web of silence: imprint
which conceals our fury,
how we fought each other to the ashes
to keep clinging to each other.
The imprint which conceals our resignation,
how we infused the heavens in each other
in order to annihilate each other.

───────────

To believe in Nothingness
more than in eternal
movements in the cosmos
is yet another faith.
I lend you
my lips, beloved,
pull down Silence on them.

The order of Nothingness
is yet another order
as long as I can
formulate it.
Beloved, pull down
Silence on my lips,
the only thing that lasts.

The amount of silence
in Silence,
the amount of nothingness
in Nothing : provinces
within the mute
realm of Remainders,
always constant.
And to get there : road
across the cinders
into summer.
Your bones
in the earth : stars
in space rejoice.
Spots of life.

Notes on the Poets

SONJA ÅKESSON (1925–1977) was one of the leading poets associated with the feminist movement in the sixties. She was for some time married to the 'concrete' poet Jarl Hammarberg who subsequently changed his name to 'Hammarberg-Åkesson'. The combination of a fine lyrical talent, mainly in the autobiographical vein, and a hard-hitting satirical invention made her, with Sandro Key-Åberg, the most formidable poetic investigator of Swedish customs and ideologies of her time.

TOBIAS BERGGREN (b. 1939) is in the forefront of the most recent developments of Swedish poetry. He has published five volumes of poetry. His Marxist convictions are embodied in a diction displaying a peculiar union of influences from Eliot and Gunnar Ekelöf.

LARS FORSSELL (b. 1928) is without doubt the most versatile poet of his generation. As poet, dramatist, critic, novelist, translator and song-writer he has no equal in Sweden; the only possible comparison is with his Danish near-contemporary Klaus Rifbjerg. His poetry combines erudition with personal confessions, political involvement with theatrical detachment. A native of Stockholm, he received a B.A. from Augustana College, Rock Island, Illinois. He is a member of the Swedish Academy.

GÖSTA FRIBERG (b. 1938) has slowly gained a solid reputation for his 'ccosophical' poetry which is lyrical, understated and to the point. He has translated American Indian poetry and has assimilated other influences from primitive art and culture. He has more recently shown a great talent for comical science fiction poetry.

MAJKEN JOHANSSON (b. 1930) was a celebrated member of the so-called 'southern school of poetry' (*Lundaskolan*) in the fifties. Her intellectual and demanding poetry shows affinities with Marianne Moore, Gertrude Stein (whom she has celebrated in her poetry) and Samuel Beckett. She later joined the Salvation Army, but her poetry has still retained its dark intensity even in her most evangelical moods.

INGEMAR LECKIUS (b. 1928) published his earlier works under the name of Ingemar Gustafson. His grave, pregnant poetry encapsulates mystical and religious ideas—he is a convert to Roman Catholicism—but also a humane identification with the oppressed and the suffering. He has only recently started to gain the recognition he deserves: a generous selection of his poetry has been published and he was awarded two prestigious literary prizes. His life-long interest in surrealist art—in particular in congenial poet-painters like Michaux or Matta—is reflected in the poems on Klee and Dubuffet. He is well-known as a translator of French, Spanish and African literature.

LARS NORÉN (b. 1943) is after some ten volumes of poetry and two novels a major figure among younger Swedish authors. His poetry, violent and hallucinatory at first, is now more quiet and introspective in mood.

PETER ORTMAN (b. 1938) has published five books of poetry. Satire and self-analysis are the two poles between which his poetry moves, in a highly personal, neo-dadaist style.

JAN ÖSTERGREN (b. 1940) used to be a gallery owner and an art dealer. Five volumes of his natural and sensitive poetry have appeared in the last five years. He has translated Marcel Duchamp and Jerome Rothenberg.

GÖRAN PALM (b. 1931), the well-known literary and social critic, is a satirical poet of great force and seriousness. His book on working-conditions in the Swedish electrical firm of L. M. Ericsson has recently been translated and is published by Cambridge University Press.

GÖRAN PRINTZ-PÅHLSON (b. 1931), literary critic and poet, is perhaps best remembered for his study of modern Swedish poetry published in 1958, *Solen i spegeln* ('The Sun in the Mirror'). For the last twenty years he has lived mainly abroad, first in the U.S.A. and later in Cambridge, England, where he is a Fellow of Clare Hall.

LASSE SÖDERBERG (b. 1931) lived in France and Spain for many years. His exquisite poetry, closely aligned to the French and Latin-American surrealism he has expertly translated, is still waiting for the recognition it deserves. Together with Ingemar Leckius he translated Leopold Senghor, the Senegalese poet and president.

GÖRAN SONNEVI (b. 1939) is a major force and influence among younger Swedish poets. His pure and warm, highly musical diction is, somewhat miraculously, able to combine intensely personal statements with an abstract Marxist critical vocabulary.

TOMAS TRANSTRÖMER (b. 1931) is the most widely read and translated of these poets in the English-speaking world. His highly original and artfully wrought poetry has been translated by Robert Bly, Robin Fulton and many others. He was trained as a psychologist and worked for many years with juvenile delinquents at a borstal in the south of Sweden.

JACQUES WERUP (b. 1947) is the youngest of the poets included. Like Majken Johansson, Printz-Påhlson and Jan Östergren he is a native of Malmö in the south of Sweden. A former rock musician, he has published three volumes of poetry and two novels. (The translators do not share the judgement implicit in his poem against Tranströmer, even if they admire the force of his invectives.)

Acknowledgements

The work on this anthology has been facilitated by a generous grant from the Anglo-Swedish Literary Foundation and by encouragement from the Swedish Institute in Stockholm and the Swedish Embassy in London. We thank these institutions, as we thank individuals who have shown interest and offered helpful suggestions. In addition to those Swedish poets who were consulted, we wish to mention Richard Burns and Judy Moffet. We are also grateful to the Columbia Translation Center, New York, who selected the anthology as recipient of one of their awards for 1978. We thank Professor Richard Vowles for permission to reprint his translation of Göran Printz-Påhlson's 'Joe Hill in Prison', which first appeared in *The Literary Review*, IX:2, 1965-66. The translation of Göran Printz-Påhlson's 'Turing Machine' first appeared in *Adam*, nos. 304-5-6. Some of the other translations have appeared in *The Greenfield Review*, *Modern Poetry in Translation*, *Poetry and Audience* and *Poetry Nation Review*.

We thank the following authors and publishers for permission to translate poems included in this anthology:

Rabén & Sjögrens förlag, Stockholm, for Sonja Åkesson's 'Ett brev' from *Jag bor i Sverige*, 1966.

Tobias Berggren and Albert Bonniers förlag, Stockholm, for 'I berget II', 'Dikt från Gotland' and 'Dikt om tiden, vid havet' from *Resor i din tystnad*, 1976.

Lars Forssell and Albert Bonniers förlag for 'Den svenska sommaren' from *Ändå*, 1968.

Gösta Friberg and Albert Bonniers förlag for 'Ingen', 'Dövstumshuset', 'Växandet' and 'Vägen' from *Växandet*, 1976.

Majken Johansson and Albert Bonniers förlag for 'Ett hus av Gertrude Stein' and 'Demonerna' from *Buskteater*, 1952; 'Till de föregående', 'René Descartes', 'Liten dialektik för poeter', 'Utflykt' from *I grund och botten*, 1956; 'Gertrude Stein again', 'En betraktelse' and 'Elegi vid en grav' from *Andens undanflykt*, 1958; 'Trappuppgång' and 'Nostalgiskt brev till G. P.-P.' from *Omtal*, 1969.

Ingemar Leckius and Albert Bonniers förlag for 'Familjeliv' and 'På en annan Planet' from *Bumerang*, 1952; 'Mirobolus Makadam & Co' from *Den hemliga metern*, 1956; 'Magister Caput', 'Tungomålstalarna' and 'Scintilla animae' from *Ravin av ljus*, 1960; 'Paul Klee', 'Lidandets voyörer', 'Metafysik' and 'Till en zenmunk' from *Lasarus bröder*, 1964; 'I öknen går de vilda fåren' from *I öknen går de vilda fåren*, 1968.

Lars Norén and Albert Bonniers förlag for 'Solitär dikt' and 'Syringe' from *Solitära dikter*, 1972; 'Onsdagen den 17 oktober' from *Dagliga och nattliga dikter*, 1974.

Lars Norén and Författarförlaget, Gothenburg, for '26 ord om Flandern', 'Från Dresden', 'Jag bränner min lampa på ängen', 'Idag, harmonins raseri', 'Afton',

'Vägarnas klot', 'Allusion', 'Slutdikt', 'Slutsats' and 'Augusti' from Viltspeglar, 1972.

Peter Ortman and Albert Bonniers förlag for 'Nollnoll vad är det' and 'Vissa dagar' from Berättelsen om Nollnoll Noll, 1975; 'Ingenting särskilt', 'Realism', 'Skaffa mörkare glas' and 'En mycket gammal man' from En passage, 1976.

Jan Östergren and Bo Cavefors Bokförlag, Lund, for '(orden)', '(kärleken)' and '(döden)' from Indiansommar, 1976.

Göran Palm and P. A. Norstedts & Söners förlag, Stockholm, for 'På detta klot' from Världen ser dig, 1964.

Göran Printz-Påhlson and Albert Bonniers förlag for 'Exempel 5 & 7' from Dikter för ett barn i vår tid, 1956; 'Sånger ur Gradiva', 'Människotillverkat monstrum', 'Sir Charles Babbage' and 'Joe Hill' from Gradiva och andra dikter, 1966.

Image förlag, Malmö, and Leif Thomsen's printing press, Copenhagen, for Göran Printz-Påhlson's 'Broendal' from Resan mellan poesi och poesi, 1955.

Lasse Söderberg and Wahlström & Widstrands förlag, Stockholm, for 'Fruktans huvudstad' from Akrobaterna, 1955.

Göran Sonnevi and Albert Bonniers förlag for 'Landskapet', 'Sjö och tystnad', 'Februari: abstrakt uppvaknande' and 'Outfört' from Outfört, 1960; 'Abstrakt värld' from Abstrakta dikter, 1963; 'Tomrum som faller' and 'Jävla fitta' from Ingrepp-modeller, 1965; 'Vill du komma in och ta en mössa på dig' from Och nu, 1967; 'Efter sju magra år' from Det gäller oss, 1969; 'Det måste gå' from Det måste gå, 1970; 'En mor står', 'Mozart-variationer', 'Die Zeit ist buchstabengenau' and 'Hölderlin' from Det omöjliga, 1975.

Tomas Tranströmer and Albert Bonniers förlag for 'Östersjöar III' from Östersjöar, 1975.

Jacques Werup and Albert Bonniers förlag for 'Tranströmer och vi andra' from Ett å två å tre å fyr!, 1971; "Jag kunde lika gärna aka nagon annanstans" from Tiden i Malmö, på jorden, 1974; 'Fläckar, hot' and 'Fläckar, tystnad' from Fläckar av liv, 1977.